...a real page t~~urner~~ ...~~ring~~s true to me, having grown up in the Midwest. I stayed up most of the night reading and found myself in awe of the human spirit which, like the hollyhocks, endures. I hope to read more of this author.

—Linda M Dix, A.B., LL.BE, J.D.
Attorney, Theater Arts Administrator,
and Non-Profit Administrator
Honolulu, Hawaii

This memoir about an amazingly dysfunctional Midwest family offers a vivid mix of infidelities, abuse, murder, alcoholism, religious fervor, psychotic episodes, and unwanted pregnancies. Despite the often unmanageable behaviors of family members, there is a subtext of love, close family ties, and with some, brokenness. You hope and pray they will make it!

—David Palmer
Publisher of *One Day at a Time*
Little Rock, Arkansas

This is an inspiring story of a young mother's determination to create a happy environment for her children in the midst of chaos, dysfunction, and evil. The resulting production of a daughter with her same strength and positive characteristics gives the reader hope that our lives do not have to be destroyed by the choices/actions of the detrimental people in our lives.

—Jane Greer
Mother and grandmother
Little Rock, Arkansas

A true, thought-provoking story of a girl growing up in middle-class America. Makes one wonder if there is any such thing as normal. It does reveal what the human spirit can overcome. I thoroughly enjoyed the story and could not put it down.

—Jamie Dunn
Former teacher, public librarian
Kansas City, Missouri

It isn't surprising that the author became a very caring, talented, and highly honored gifted and talented education teacher and mentor. I believe she has the sensitivity and love for her own children and students that was missing in her own childhood.

—Kay Howell
RN, interior designer
Little Rock, Arkansas

Hollyhocks
on the fence

CARYN WELLES

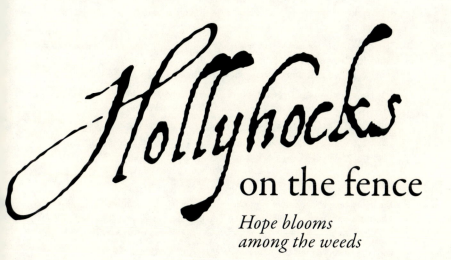

on the fence

*Hope blooms
among the weeds*

TATE PUBLISHING & *Enterprises*

Hollyhocks on the Fence
Copyright © 2009 by Caryn Welles. All rights reserved.

No part of this publication may be reproduced, stored in a retrieval system or transmitted in any way by any means, electronic, mechanical, photocopy, recording or otherwise without the prior permission of the author except as provided by USA copyright law.

Scripture quotations marked "NIV" are taken from the *Holy Bible, New International Version* ®, Copyright © 1973, 1978, 1984 by International Bible Society. Used by permission of Zondervan Publishing House. All rights reserved.

This novel is a work of fiction. However, several names, descriptions, entities, and incidents included in the story are based on the lives of real people.

The opinions expressed by the author are not necessarily those of Tate Publishing, LLC.

Published by Tate Publishing & Enterprises, LLC
127 E. Trade Center Terrace | Mustang, Oklahoma 73064 USA
1.888.361.9243 | www.tatepublishing.com

Tate Publishing is committed to excellence in the publishing industry. The company reflects the philosophy established by the founders, based on Psalm 68:11,
"The Lord gave the word and great was the company of those who published it."

Book design copyright © 2009 by Tate Publishing, LLC. All rights reserved.
Cover design by Leah LeFlore
Interior design by Nathan Harmony

Published in the United States of America

ISBN: 978-1-61566-072-8
1. Biography & Autobiography: Personal Memoirs
2. Family & Relationships: Abuse: General
09.09.09

Dedication

I dedicate this book in remembrance of my mother, whose beauty, heroism, and dedication to God helped my brothers and me celebrate life in spite of the traumatic childhood we encountered at the hands of those who should have protected us against the evil one. "Every memory of you has served as a beacon of light in my journey through all of the stages of my life, and for that, I am eternally grateful."

I will repay you for the years the locusts have eaten...
　　　　　Joel 2:25 (NIV Study Bible)

Introduction

Early in my teaching career, a young boy whom I will call Scotty quietly tiptoed into my second-grade classroom on a warm fall day and sat in the next-to-the-last seat in the first row. That wouldn't have been unusual, except that it was the first day of school, and students usually don't arrive in their new classroom an hour late without supplies or parents in tow.

All of the other students had introduced themselves to the rest of the class, and I thought it was appropriate to let Scotty introduce himself as well. It was then that I questioned the sensitivity of that decision because Scotty's lip began to quiver as he slowly turned to face the class. His movements were stiff, and he grimaced in pain as he pushed himself up from his seat. I immediately sensed that something was seriously wrong. When he turned to face me, I noticed several large, fresh bruises covering his arms and a hand mark on the side of his face that was beginning to turn blue.

Later on in the year, Scotty brought a note up to my puppet, Margaret, telling her in his childish handwriting that he needed help because his teenage half brother had been sexually abusing him for as long as he could remember. My heart broke as I remembered the emotional childhood abuse that my brothers and I endured and realized that this waif of a child had probably met evil face-to-face before he walked through the door of his new school.

It took me months to help him break down his walls of distrust and apprehension, but eventually, with the counselor's help, he began to smile and play with the others. His schoolwork improved so much by the end of the school year that his name appeared on the honor roll, and his parents regularly attended parent-teacher meetings. His eighteen-year-old brother had a choice to either join the army or spend time in jail, so he left Arkansas in shame and joined the army. As far as I know, he never returned to Arkansas to force his will on Scotty again, and his little brother was able to live out the rest of his childhood years without having to endure that kind of fear again.

There were many "Scottys" throughout my rather lengthy teaching career, and I felt a great responsibility to try to relieve each of their fears and give them hopes that their future lives would be a lot better than the one they were enduring at that time. I relived the pain of my own childhood each time one of these children crossed my path and wondered how many more were being traumatized behind closed doors. My abusive relatives did not succeed in breaking my spirit as a result of their mental and physical abuse, nor did they quench my spirit of love for others; but what they did do was make me more alert to the signs of childhood abuse in my own students so that I could find ways to make their lives a little more palatable while they were part of my ever-widening family of pupils. In that way, I feel that the trauma of my childhood has worked for good because I have been able to reach many hurting and lost children through my own experiences with my father's wildly dysfunctional family.

I pray that my book, *Hollyhocks on the Fence*, will give hope to the hopeless and optimism for the future to the hurting, because the consequences of evil can be overcome by faith in God and a realization that he is bigger than all of the torturous memories that threaten to destroy the lives of an innumerable army of adults who have lived through childhood abuse.

Chapter One

It had been a day filled with sunshine and light winds, but a canopy of clouds raced across the sky by late afternoon, painting the neighbor's backyard in an almost eerie shade of grayish green. I had just finished baking Bob's favorite dessert of apple dumplings when a telephone call jolted me from the feelings of heaviness that had nagged at me throughout the day. I had shrugged them off several times and decided that I would experience these "downer" days, as I called them, until I could accept my new retirement status.

It had been almost a year since I turned in my notice to the school board announcing that I would not be returning, but I had not experienced the joy of retirement that I hoped I would. I looked forward to the day when I could begin my second career as a writer, but being a successful writer involves self-discipline, which I discovered is not one of my strong suits. I had won several writing awards in the areas of short story and poetry during my career-oriented days, which encouraged me to consider writing about my unbelievably dysfunctional family. The right time to begin my story, however, never seemed to present itself until I received the phone call from my cousin Catherine informing me that her mother, Aunt Edna, had passed away in the night and that they would like it if my brothers and I could attend her funeral. My aunt was Mother's confidant and best friend who shared her most intimate secrets, and I often prayed that she would agree to be my mother if my own mother's health gave out during one of her many episodes with her weakening heart.

After hanging up the phone, I realized that I had to write our story because my brothers and I are the last ones to remember the truth because our only cousin on my father's side of the family had not experienced the terror that was often inflicted on Patrick, Michael, and me. I often wondered as a child why nobody else came to my two brothers' and my aid during our times of terror at my Grandmother Gus's house, but I guess my father's side of the family kept their secrets well hidden. When we became teenagers and weren't forced to stay overnight with Grandmother Gus any longer, we informed our mother of the more sordid incidences that occurred while she was in the hospital during her many unplanned and painful episodes, and tears of remorse welled up in her eyes. Afterwards, our mother must have been unable to hold these secrets in her heart because Aunt Edna informed me during a phone conversation several months before she died that she was so sorry that none of the Polks knew of the abuse and were therefore unable to protect us from the evil that seemed to rear its ugly head nearly every time we entered the doors of Grandmother Gus's house. That seems like a long time ago, but for some reason I find it necessary to pay them back for those stolen childhood years by writing about our experiences in that two-story house that has long since been torn down.

My husband and I moved to Nashville, Tennessee, in the spring of 1965, after he received his transfer papers assigning him to a new position with a government law enforcement agency. I accepted a second-grade teaching position with the Nashville Public School System and was looking forward to our new life. It was a rather frightening experience for both of us because we had never been away from our families and friends. However, we soon met other young couples who shared our interests and began enjoying the exciting activities that Nashville had to offer people our age.

Spelunking in the caves around Murfreesboro and canoeing in the whitewater rivers across Tennessee became a weekend obsession. Luckily, we didn't have to discover the state by ourselves because we became friends with a couple whom I met through my teaching assignment. Through them, we were able to appease our desire to explore the great outdoors.

David was a tall, lanky biology student whose uncombed tufts of blond hair gave him the appearance of a molting crane. Helen, his wife, was the perfect example of a Peabody education department alum with extremely high intelligence and a natural curiosity for life. Other than her bleached blond hair, she seemed completely detached from most worldly influences. Neither one of them appeared athletic, but beyond their rather fragile appearances, we learned how to enjoy nature through them in ways that we had never experienced before. Their appetite for outdoor activities rivaled ours, and we became inseparable on the weekends that my husband wasn't working.

Several weeks after an especially adventurous overnight, late summer campout, we discovered that I was pregnant and were overjoyed at the thought of becoming a family. I decided not to reapply for a teaching position that next fall because my due date would have interfered with my teaching responsibilities. Besides, the rumor was that we would be transferred to the Washington, D.C., detail within the next six months, and we wanted to be free to move when our orders arrived.

My husband had been called to leave town on an extended assignment by the end of November, and I decided to fly home before the window of opportunity closed as my pregnancy progressed. I had missed my family and friends terribly and welcomed the opportunity to reconnect with them and talk about old times and plans for the future baby. My dreams of a pleasant visit were cut short, however, by the death of my grandmother Gus, who always seemed to instinctively know when to negatively disrupt my life.

She had been a negative force throughout my childhood when she played havoc during our holiday dinners and demanded that her personal needs be placed before any others in the family. In spite of Grandmother Gus's less than perfect disposition, however, my father and his two sisters harbored a fierce devotion to their matriarchal parent and treated her as if she had been an honorable role model instead of the dangerously fiendish authority figure my brothers and I dealt with.

Dark memories of her menacing laughter still made me shudder as I recalled the times when she and Aunt Maxine delighted in my reaction to the coconut head that they hid in the shadows of the stairwell or their stories of ghosts who walked the gloomy halls at night. Grandmother Gus was especially caustic toward me, and I never could figure out why unless she just didn't want another girl in the family after my cousin, Candace, was born fifteen years earlier. Also, my father always left Patrick, Michael, and me with Gus whenever our mother had to be rushed to the hospital, and I figured that she was afraid our mother would die and she would be left with the responsibility of raising us three children. Perhaps the prospect of that situation was more than she could fathom since she didn't seem to exhibit any natural parenting skills. She had farmed her own children out to be raised by her brother and his wife, so it was highly unlikely that she had honed her mothering abilities that late in life.

I was always grateful when God answered my childish prayers and restored Mother to her rightful maternal position so that we could return to our own well-run and clean home. My father never seemed to bond to his own wife and children as profoundly as he did to his own mother, so his lack of enthusiasm for fatherhood in general encouraged his extended family to treat my brothers and me with a disdain that was hard for us to understand.

All these thoughts were shattering my hopes of a well-earned visit with my brothers and mother, and before my plane landed in Kansas City, I had to consciously take note of the positives in my life and accept my childhood memories as though they were no longer significant to the present.

My plane arrived at the Kansas City airport in the middle of an extremely aggressive winter thunderstorm, and I felt slightly queasy as I fell into line behind the other passengers who were busily opening the overhead bins and extracting a myriad of bulging suitcases from their tightly packed crevices. It seemed like an eternity before the human chain of mannerly passengers began to spill out of the open door and I was once again able to breathe fresh air. I didn't want to have to wag a heavy suitcase with me, so I mentally made a note of where the pickup point would be for our flight and proceeded to follow the signs that pointed me in the right direction. My mother and Michael were planning to meet me by the luggage area, so I was trying to pick them out in the teeming mass that seemed to be converging on the baggage like an enormous flock of squawking, ill-tempered birds.

Just as I began to feel lightheaded from the body heat and roar of the crowd, I spied Mother and Michael walking toward me as if I was the only person in the terminal. They were grinning as if they shared a common secret and simultaneously wrapped me in their arms as if to shield me from the multitude of passengers who were searching for their suitcases. Mother looked tired and relieved at the same time as she kissed my cheek and squeezed my hand in hers. Michael took my luggage check and quickly found my two suitcases with the bright red ribbon tied onto the handle of each.

Mother walked between Michael and me and occasionally leaned on one of us to regain her balance as we found our way to my brother's car. I shot a questioning look at Michael over Mother's head, but she must have seen my glance because she quickly informed me that she had been losing her balance on occasion lately after allowing herself to become overtired. I worried about her health, but God had chosen to let her live many years beyond her doctor's predictions, and I was grateful for any quality of life that she had left. She didn't seem upset that Grandmother Gus had passed away but that we would have to be thrust into the midst of the Baxter family dynamics during such emotion-packed circumstances.

Aunt Stella had been the one who called my mother to inform her of Gus's death and remained stoic until my father took the phone. At that time, sobs of sorrow racked her body to the point of alarming my father, and he immediately jumped into the car and met her at the nursing home where the coroner had pronounced Grandmother Gus dead earlier that morning. Mother immediately called my two brothers to inform them of our grandmother's demise and when the viewing would be held. I knew that this would be another visit I would never forget.

Michael quietly drove us toward our parents' home while Mother and I chatted about my life in Nashville. We did not mention anything about the funeral arrangements until we pulled into the driveway and saw that Aunt Stella had already beaten us there. Mother quickly informed us about the visitation so that our aunt wouldn't think that we weren't interested in the activities that threatened to once again steal our joy. Michael parked the car in the well-organized garage, and we all resolutely climbed the stairs to face our father and his grieving sister.

I knew my mother would be asked to prepare the food for those guests who would attend the funeral, and because her health had declined through the years, I felt that she needed my assistance. It had been my mother who had prepared most of the holiday meals for my father's family throughout her married life, and it seemed appropriate somehow for her to fix the final meal that would usher my grandmother on to her final destination into eternity, wherever that might be.

My younger brother, Michael, and I were assigned the responsibility of picking up our older brother, Patrick, at the airport the following afternoon after my arrival. He was not at all happy about returning to Kansas City under those circumstances, but after he found out that Aunt Stella was paying for his plane fare, he decided that becoming an opportunist was appropriate for the situation and that he could complete the art job he was working on after he returned to Dallas. He contacted several of his gay friends who had graduated with him from the Art Center in Kansas City, and they had agreed to meet on the weekend. Since Patrick's plane fare had already been taken care of, this seemed to be the perfect time to plan a reunion party with them after he paid his respects to Dad's family.

Michael had been drinking most of the next day before he picked me up, and our journey to the airport was not without some frightening moments. I breathed a sigh of relief when I spotted our older brother in front of the terminal leaning against the handle of his suitcase. He looked sharp as usual in his light wool, navy blue sports jacket over immaculately pressed, khaki-colored slacks. I felt the tension easing from my body because I knew he would convince our little brother to give him the wheel and safely deposit us at our final destination. My relief was short-lived, however, because it did not take long to realize that Patrick had been drinking throughout the flight.

He greeted me with his usual sarcastic humor by asking if I "had eaten the whole thing" as he observed my widening girth and ample thighs. His unsteady demeanor and bloodshot eyes belied the fact that he wasn't in any better shape than Mike to drive us home. I swallowed my anger at our dilemma because I figured that each of us in our own way was trying to detach from the memories that were sure to surface as we faced the family from which we had tried so hard to escape. I was the only one who wasn't detaching by experiencing an alcoholic funk, however, and offered to drive us back to the house and safety.

Without questioning the sanity of their decision, both brothers immediately decided that Michael should drive. His occupation was an over-the-road truck driver, and in their rather questionable states of mind, they agreed that his experience would override his condition. I surprised myself by spewing out several caustic words, but they seemed amused at my lack of self-control and remained staunch in their choice of drivers for our cross-town adventure. In spite of my pleading and threatening to tell

Mother how drunk they were, they both ignored me and proceeded to carry on their own personal conversation as if I weren't in the car at all.

Several hours passed, and we were no closer to our parents' home than we had been when we started out. Kansas City is an enormously diverse town with neighborhoods that are dangerous for strangers at any time of the day or night, and it would be very easy to find yourself in a compromising situation if you didn't know where you were going. As we drove through pockets of deteriorating neighborhoods in various stages of decay, we continued to search for familiar surroundings while my brothers stopped periodically to boost their morale with more liquor. My older brother declared that there was a very strong possibility that we could all get killed by a drug dealer if we did not find our way out of this part of town before dark. His wish was to be completely drunk if that happened, and he was well on his way to being just that.

By the time we arrived home, it was early the next morning. My mother had stayed up waiting for us and was so completely overcome with relief when she saw us come into the front door she tearfully hugged each one of us and ushered us to our bedrooms as Mike slipped out to return to his home and family. Her goal was not to wake our father, or he would have most assuredly made an already uncomfortable situation even more unpalatable.

Each of us slept soundly and woke up to the delicious smell of coffee and pancakes. I padded down the hall in my fluffy house shoes and was delighted to see my mother standing over the stove in her long, pink, cotton nightgown and robe. She looked much younger than her fifty-five years, and that amazed me because of the health issues that seemed to dog her throughout her life. I stood there silently for a few moments watching the woman who enriched all of our lives so much.

Suddenly, she turned and ran toward me with outstretched arms and planted a kiss on my cheek before I had time to tell her how glad I was to be there. Her familiar peach scent took me back to my childhood when I wrote a paper about how good my mother smelled. It would have been a perfect morning except for my father's untimely intrusion into the kitchen.

He mumbled something like, "Hi, Sis. How's it going?" and then grunted something inaudible when I told him how sorry I was to hear about his mother's death. He barely acknowledged my brother's presence as Patrick stumbled into the kitchen several minutes later with an obvious hangover and a surly attitude that was the result of years of animosity between the two. Mother instructed us to sit down at the table while she served us breakfast as she had done throughout our childhood years.

The crisp, white, eyelet curtains trimmed with a red ribbon framed the bay window that opened onto a patio that was built around an enormous oak tree. Under the aging tree sat a stone poodle serenely staring up into the barren branches that were swaying in the wintry air. A plastic, multi-colored tablecloth covering the oval kitchen table formed the perfect background for the white plates stacked high with steaming pancakes dripping with maple syrup and melting butter.

As my brother and I savored the delicious meal, our dad, Victor, nervously paced the floor and checked the clock every few minutes to see if the time was near to depart for his mother's viewing at the funeral home. Mother had told him to go ahead and meet his sister so they could finalize the funeral arrangements and meet guests who would be arriving throughout the day to visit with their family, but he refused and demanded that Mother leave the dirty dishes in the sink and ride with him. We assured her that we would clean up the kitchen and that Mike would pick us up a little later and bring us with him to the visitation. I made Patrick promise that he would not be tempted to join our little brother in drinking before the viewing because of my condition, and he agreed.

Several hours and several beers later, Michael appeared at the front door without his family and ready to attack whatever situation we might confront at the funeral home that day. He even agreed to let our older brother drive in return for us letting him drink on the way to the viewing. Patrick and I both knew that he needed this boost to his courage and secretly wished that we too could take something to mollify the situation. Underneath his fearless exterior lived a very small and fearful boy whose memory was cluttered with the events that occurred during our visits to Gus's two-story house, and the damage from those incidences affected him much deeper than he would ever admit.

We three took a seat in the second row of the visitors' room and watched as acquaintances and members of the family came and went. We did not mingle with the rest of the crowd because in our detachment we somehow felt less threatened by our surroundings. We had expected to see our parents in the viewing area, but someone informed us that they had seen them talking earlier with the priest who was going to lead the service the next day and that they were expecting them to enter the room at any minute. In the meantime, I was pleased to be sitting with the most handsome young men in the room and reveled in the fact that they were part of my immediate family.

My brothers had inherited our mother's, Ramona's, blond hair and dimpled chin and my father's well-built frame. My appearance was a combination of the best of both parents because I had inherited a mane of dark, auburn hair and full lips that opened to reveal a set of teeth as white as my mother's favorite teacup. However, my usually slender body was beginning to fill out with the advancing pregnancy, and the protruding bump under my black and white hound's-tooth maternity top threatened to alter my dress size forever.

As the actors in our story entered onto the set of the funeral home, I began to record the story of our childhood onto the tablet in my mind. It is only now as I recall those memories that I can write them down without any fear of reprisal from other members of my father's family. I reach back to those days of wholesome family entertainment and solid Christian values where life was met on life's terms, and as children, our needs were considerably less important than the needs of those adults who were responsible for our well-being.

Chapter Two

The McGuilley funeral home had once been the most luxurious of its kind in Kansas City, but by the year 1966, those days had long since passed. The dark curtains surrounding the family viewing room hung in opulent folds as if they were the backdrop for a major theatrical production, and the lowered lighting created an air of mysterious undertones. The overpowering scent of roses mingled with an indistinguishable musty smell set the stage for my grandmother Gus's funeral. A white satin pillow cushioned my grandmother's head as she lay quietly in a mahogany casket fit for a queen. Shadows played across her face, making it appear as though her eyelashes fluttered occasionally, and a smile seemed to tug at her tightly pursed lips as though she was amused at the activities surrounding her.

An assortment of guests and family mingled around the body, and occasionally there would be a guest or two who would drop in to sign the guest registry and whisper a few words of condolence to members of my family.

Several well-dressed men with swarthy complexions filed in, signed the guest book after placing their boutonnieres on Gus's chest, and quietly left as they nodded a silent good-bye to my aunt Stella.

Two young, attractive nursing home caretakers approached the casket and stared down at their former patient with obvious disdain in their eyes. My grandmother had been one of their most difficult patients who had made their lives miserable by hiding her teeth, throwing food, and refusing to let them change her sheets after soiling her bed. The girls nervously giggled at their boldness as they quickly backed out into the chilling wintry air to avoid any conversation with Gus's relatives. They were sure that their hasty retreat had gone unnoticed, but it was not in my aunt's nature to overlook any indiscretion whether obvious or not. She borrowed a pen from the funeral director and wrote herself a note to call the nursing home the next Monday and report the poor care her mother had received while in their facility.

My cousin's husband gave his respects and quickly retreated to a brocade-covered chair that was positioned well beyond the others in the funeral party. He seemed to observe the rest of the family in a rather amused and detached fashion, as if his social position set him apart from the common man. His successful dental practice and extravagant lifestyle had given him an aura of self-confidence and good taste as well as a general disdain for others who had not achieved his status in life. Black, curly hair and expressive brown eyes completed an overpowering persona that prompted feelings of awe in most everyone who came into contact with him.

A small commotion near the side door indicated that someone else had entered the room, and as expected, my father strode in and walked directly to his mother's casket. Almost immediately, a long-legged and rather heavily made-up young lady sauntered up to him from somewhere in the back and placed her hand on his shoulder. As she whispered words that were only meant for him, Victor's usual facial tic became more pronounced. He motioned for her to sit in the chairs intended for family members and stared into the motionless face of a person who had once called herself his mother. Only a hint of emotion played behind my father's gray-blue eyes as he turned and appeared to read the messages on the flower arrangements that surrounded the casket.

As my mother quietly followed him to pay her last respects, no one bothered to acknowledge her, nor did she seem to care because she had nothing in common with his family. There was an innocence about her as she carried herself with a sense of dignity and ladylike composure. Her soft blond hair framed a face with delicate features and well-formed, full lips. A dusting of soft pink rouge kissed the cheeks of her fragile, China-like complexion, and she shuddered as she glanced over at the brazen young woman who had made her presence known only moments before. Ramona wore an expensive, long-sleeved, silk shirtwaist dress that Aunt Stella had given her for the funeral. Her full figure and small waist were accentuated by a black velvet belt, and a single strand of pearls added the perfect accent to a tasteful yet unassumingly elegant outfit.

As she sat down next to my father, neither one said a single word to the other. There seemed to be no connection between them at all as they stared at the casket and silently reveled in their own thoughts. Occasionally, Ramona would shift in her seat, and Victor would scowl at her as if to reprimand her for entering his private personal space.

The only other person sitting on the front row was the young woman who obviously knew my father very well, and it was her leg that touched his thigh, not my mother's. Other members of the family were obviously used to this side of Victor and in fact seemed to smugly welcome his actions as a way to pay Ramona back for her nonconformity to their lifestyle. The young lady was not acknowledged by anyone else in the funeral party besides the dentist who smiled warmly at her as she cast an occasional furtive glance over her shoulder as if anticipating the sudden appearance of an unwanted guest.

Maxine, the youngest of Gus's children, continually moved in and out of the group as she looked for her missing husband, Bill. She was diminutive in size and walked with an easy but determined gait. Size wasn't a negative asset for her, however, because she made up for it by a scathingly hurtful ability to cut others down with her gift of a plethora of negative words. This attribute became more pronounced as her body reacted to the liquor that was part of her daily routine.

Both she and Bill were partners in a sordid lifestyle, which included verbal and physical abuse and a penchant for landing in jail after their frequent, late-night binges. Most jail visits were short-time incidences, however, because my uncle Bill was a longtime member in good standing of an elite team of firefighters in the Kansas City area. His reputation for bravery was well known among the other firemen and policemen throughout the city. A slap on the wrist and a rehearsed warning was the extent of the punishment either one of the couple ever received after each drunken incident. It was understood among those who knew Bill that his bravery was bought with a pint of whiskey and that his position at the end of the ladder truck was perfect for someone who felt no fear of the inevitable hellish infernos that most certainly lay ahead.

Aunt Maxine did not resemble her brothers or sister physically because they were dark-haired and olive-skinned, and she was blessed with a mass of blond curls and eyes the color of jade. But beyond this, she had inherited a rather wide nose and close-set eyes that reminded one of a mixed breed of puppy. It was whispered among the elite of the small town in which she was born that Maxine bore a striking resemblance to the doctor who practiced medicine in the more rural areas around Rich Hill. Because my grandmother was not known to be committed to her deteriorating marriage, there was much speculation as to whom the real father might be, and no doubt a few nervous, married suitors breathed a sigh of relief when Gus ultimately decided to leave town.

Kate Hepburn was my aunt's heroine, and she dressed in the latest fashionable slacks that were the rage inspired by the famous actress. Silk blouses and fake fur coats filled her clothes closet, but it was the enormous selection of stark white gloves that set her apart from other style-conscious women of the time. Her natural penchant for mimicking the latest fads in the clothing industry simply had to be inborn because her upbringing had not personally introduced her to those people who traveled in fashion-conscious circles. Aunt Maxine had also not been affected by the poverty-stricken lifestyle that her older brothers and sister had grown up in because she was the only one of Gus's children who had been allowed to accompany her mother to Kansas City after her father died and Grandmother Gus remarried.

The other three children barely had enough clothing to keep them warm during the winter months. They attended school barefooted in the fall and spring, and when the first frost coated the dried cornstalks, they wore used shoes donated to their aunt by the local church. They had been left in Appleton City with Gus's brother and diabetic wife, who made ends meet by taking in others' washing and by raising a large vegetable garden that supplemented their very sparse meals. Their existence depended on the generosity and hard work primarily of their Aunt Grace, who took on a Goliath-size job of raising her husband's niece and nephews in spite of the fact that Uncle Clyde spent most of his waking hours at the local bar visiting with the other town drunks.

It might seem that Maxine had been extremely fortunate to escape the bleak life that her siblings were left to deal with; however, life with her mother was not without its own drawbacks. She was often neglected and left to fend for herself as her mother spent her own time and energy on the continuous procession of men who came in and out of her life. Her stepfather had died from a heart attack several years after moving into the two-story house in Kansas City, and this left my grandmother free to prey upon the male population in her area of influence.

Life was without many constraints for Maxine because her mother wasn't into the pressures of motherhood and its demands on her time and money. Gus had only one rule for her daughter, and that was to avoid pregnancy at any cost. It wasn't the fact that Gus had a moral issue about her daughter having sex before marriage but that a grandchild would make her face the fact that her irresponsibility was not due to youthfulness but to a far sinister and self-serving need.

It was during one of my grandmother's searches for a new man that my aunt met her future husband, Bill. Gus's date for the evening brought along his much younger friend to visit with Maxine while he and my grandmother disappeared behind the hanging shell curtain separating the living room from the dining room, which doubled as her downstairs bedroom. My aunt and uncle sat on the front porch swing to avoid hearing Gus and her new boyfriend's passionate utterances. My uncle had brought along a flask of liquor from which they took sips as they talked well into the night. This began a courtship that ended in marriage less than four months later.

Unfortunately, Maxine did not recognize that Bill lacked the skills to be able to provide her with a stable home because he too had been raised in a family where

Christian values were considered obsolete. Her own background blinded her to the fact that in order to reach those dreams, she would have to look beyond the man who sat beside her on the swing that summer night. When the reality of her situation began to sink in, she detached from the starkness of her life by establishing a pattern of drinking that continued throughout her marriage.

She and Bill had contemplated divorce from the first week of their marriage and were horribly devastated when they learned of Maxine's pregnancy three months later. She realized that she and Bill would not be good parents but decided not to abort the baby after Gus and her sister, Stella, persuaded her to keep it in return for their promise to help her with the baby after it was born. Consequently, after the baby's birth, she bundled up her infant child, Candace, each morning and rode across town to her mother's house in a taxicab paid for by her sister.

She carried a large satchel filled with dirty clothes, soiled white gloves, and a quart of Wild Turkey. Occasionally, her satchel included a box of perm solution, which she used to fix our grandmother's hair or to glamorize others who had heard about her near-professional ability to style hair in the latest fashion. Her days were filled with endless gossip, drinking, and arguing with her sister over the neglect she displayed in the role of motherhood. Grandmother Gus was always relieved to call a taxi for Maxine at the end of each day, but many times, Candace was permitted to stay all night in a bedroom that had been set aside for her to escape the daily grind of drunken arguments that erupted between her mother and father.

Aunt Stella made sure that Grandmother Gus was well supplied with ample provisions in order to make Candace comfortable. She was generous to a fault when it came to her beloved niece, and Grandmother Gus was more than willing to accept any recompense that came her way. Perhaps in some small way, Gus felt that this exonerated her from her poor attempts at motherhood when her own daughter, Maxine, was a child; or maybe she thought that as long as she played the part of a surrogate parent, Aunt Stella would continue to shower both her and Candace with money to help her with her mounting bills.

Even though their daughter would eventually escape the cycle of verbal and substance abuse, her parents continued to display erratic behavior in titanic proportions throughout her entire life. Maxine and her husband could have been the counterparts of the infamous Bonnie and Clyde Barrow except for the fact that they were not capable of strategic thinking after four o'clock in the afternoon. This was about the time that the alcohol began to take effect on their logical thinking skills, and finding someone to fight with seemed to be the focus of their attention when Uncle Bill wasn't at the firehouse.

Several years after Candace's husband became established in his dental practice on the more affluent side of town, they received a call from Aunt Stella informing them that Maxine and Bill were in the emergency room but that she had everything under control and they didn't need to come. It was a rainy evening, and Uncle Bill had been drinking throughout the day. He had dropped onto the couch in his usual drunken stupor and was unable to run an errand to the local liquor store for his wife. After several vain attempts at arousing him from his deep sleep, my aunt picked up a heavy, ornate, metal ashtray and brought it down against his upper lip with a resounding thud. Not only did my uncle wake up, but in reaction to the pain and confusion, he knocked her out with one of his famous left hooks. The neighbors were alerted to the situation by the unusually high pitch of the screams and called the police, who took them to the emergency room to be stitched up before placing them in their usual jail cell for the night.

Aunt Stella bailed her sister out the next day but chose to leave Bill in the police station for the next several days until she was satisfied that he would not inflict any more pain on her deserving sister as retribution for knocking out his bottom and top front teeth. Uncle Bill was a forgiving sort, however, and was fit with the best false teeth his son-in-law had in stock, and all was forgiven until the next time their tempers flared over something as mundane as leaving the milk on the kitchen table or piling dirty dishes in the sink.

Several months after this incident, Maxine and Bill decided to leave Candace at Grandmother's house and ride the city bus downtown to a more expensive beer joint and restaurant than the one on the corner. It was Bill's day off, and they had been drinking throughout the day. Boredom and restlessness prompted the couple to seek entertainment outside their home, so Aunt Maxine brushed her blond curls, applied bright red lipstick to her lips, and dressed their daughter in her flannel nightclothes. They drove their car

Grandmother Gus's house, and after depositing Candace, they caught the bus that ran downtown.

Young soldiers had flooded the town for a weekend of fun and relaxation after completing a stint in basic training. The evening started out innocent enough, with Aunt Maxine dancing and toasting the young knights of the American forces, until that magical moment when the clock struck midnight and Uncle Bill decided it was time for them to leave. Aunt Maxine objected noisily as her husband grabbed her arm and proceeded to escort her out the front door. This created quite a stir among the patriotic but definitely drunk men, and one of them surprised my uncle with an uppercut, striking him squarely on his jaw. The owner was already aware of my aunt and uncle's reputation for being destructive and knew that if this fight got out of hand, his business was at stake, so he personally escorted the fun-loving couple out the back door and onto the next available bus that would take them far from him and his bar. Two of the soldiers had followed the tipsy pair, however, and had boarded the bus with the intention of rescuing the loud, fun-loving little lady and escorting her back to the party.

Almost immediately, the young soldiers began to goad my uncle into fighting both of them. To their bewilderment, however, the situation didn't seem to strike fear into the hearts of the tipsy twosome at all. In fact, my uncle calmly instructed my aunt to put on her white gloves and hit the smallest soldier in his right eye while he took control of the situation with the larger and more sober part of the pair. The altercation didn't have time to escalate out of hand, however, because the bus driver immediately stopped the bus and hailed a policeman, who promptly escorted all four of the fighting team to his waiting paddy wagon and booked them for another night in the local lockup. Another chapter had been written in Uncle Bill and Aunt Maxine's journals of drunken escapades, in which they earned the unquestionably deserved award for being two of the most frequent visitors in most of the precincts within a five-mile radius from their home. Aunt Maxine and Uncle Bill were so drunk by the time the viewing was over that my father paid a Yellow Cab to take them to their house so they wouldn't upset the visiting guests. Aunt Maxine objected to being left out of the activities but agreed to go along with her older brother and sister's wishes after they threatened her and her husband with bodily harm. It was a shame that they couldn't be included in the family activities that were usually held at our house, but whenever they were around, there was sure to be some kind of an upheaval. Both of my parents agreed that the best way to handle that situation was to eliminate the problem by leaving them out.

I remember the last time they came to Thanksgiving dinner at our house when I was ten years old. Mother had just returned from an extended hospital stint, and my father insisted that she fix dinner in spite of her condition. Dad had seen her sick so often that I believe he had grown callous to the fact that she could die from her weakened heart and never discouraged her from fixing a full holiday meal for his family. She had just taken the turkey out of the oven while I set the table when we heard a loud commotion in the side yard. We both ran to the window and looked out upon a most disturbing scene.

My uncle was holding his hand, which was encased in a full cast, and was howling in much the same way that a dying hyena might scream. My father told us the whole story later when we had a chance to ask him why Uncle Bill and Aunt Maxine didn't eat Thanksgiving dinner with us. We couldn't imagine that the situation could have been too serious because of the way the rest of his family came in and ate their meal with gusto and no concern for the welfare of their absent relatives.

After my father's family left, he told us that Uncle Bill had been drinking and was driving into our side yard much too fast to avoid hitting Stella and Dan's new Cadillac. Bill's front left fender scraped against the expensive black paint of the O'Malleys' automobile, and my aunt was ready to hit him as he stepped out of the driver's side of his much-abused vehicle. He held his damaged arm over his face to avoid being punched in the eye by Stella as Aunt Maxine screamed at her sister to leave her husband alone.

My grandmother stepped into the middle of the melee and lifted her cane over her head, bringing it down with a resounding thud against the thumb that my uncle had broken the night before in a violent bar fight. Before he had a chance to retaliate, my uncle Dan clipped him over the right eye and was getting ready to plummet the poor sot again when both my aunt and uncle jumped into their car to escape the mob mentality of the rest of their clan.

Our neighbors were elderly folks who led a rather simple life, so I'm relatively sure that their Thanksgiving holiday was given a dramatic turn as they watched the drama unfolding in their neighbors' yard. I'm thankful that they didn't call the police because many of my school friends lived in our neighborhood, and I didn't want to be talked about by the other kids in my class. It was bad enough that my father answered the door each Halloween night with a nylon stocking over his head and a ketchup-covered melon in his hands. I certainly didn't want the notoriety of having more than one relative with questionable sanity.

Aunt Maxine and Uncle Bill were married for over fifty years, but as they each approached the end of their lives, it was apparent that they only remembered a fraction of those years. Maybe it was a blessing, because when they weren't fighting they were an amazingly dysfunctional couple who seemed to complement each other on a far different level than most other people understood. It was no wonder that my brothers and I were constantly in fear of our safety around these two characters because we never knew if we were dealing with the Aunt Maxine who was hilariously funny one minute or the aunt who was caustically sarcastic the next. Uncle Bill, on the other hand, was nearly always drunk on his days off from the fire station, so we knew to make a point of staying as far away from him as possible.

A cold breeze slammed against the side of my face much later on the afternoon of the viewing, and Aunt Maxine and Uncle Bill suddenly appeared at the side entrance, walking unsteadily and smelling of cheap bourbon. As they weaved among the flower sprays, my aunt Stella shot a scathing look at them, and they belligerently made their way to the darkest corner of the room to sit under the exit sign and periodically take a swig out of a silver flask that Bill kept in the secret pocket of his favorite jacket. We were glad that they were sitting as far away from us as possible because in this way we did not have to engage in any small talk that would have fallen on their disinterested ears. We had gotten used to Bill and Maxine's aberrant ways throughout the years but did not relish the possibility of renewing our relationship with them. Their actions were the cause of many childish nightmares for my brothers and me, and we were glad that those days of catering to their whims had long since passed. Even though my brothers and I had learned to laugh at stories of their undeniably outrageous episodes, we could not overlook their nearly complete lack of positive character traits.

Chapter Three

Uncle Danny, my Aunt Stella's husband, looked uncomfortable in his Western-style-cut suit and gray Stetson hat. I always wondered why he still dressed like a cowboy since his days of working at the stock yards had long since passed. There was something about me, however, that my uncle Danny seemed to appreciate, and for this, I felt a tenderness toward him even though we never carried on much of a conversation.

His bulging stomach pushed uncomfortably against his enormous silver belt buckle. He too smelled of liquor, but the smell that surrounded him was much more expensive in nature and seemed to be working much slower to affect him physically and mentally. His left hand sported a gold ring with a diamond horseshoe, and his silk tie was centered by a diamond stud that glistened as he walked toward his wife, who by that time was talking loudly to the funeral home director.

Uncle Dan's soft leather, high-heeled cowboy boots

clicked against the polished marble floor as he strained to hear what was being said in Aunt Maxine's one-sided, animated conversation. As a once successful amateur boxer and bull buyer in the Kansas City stockyards, he still carried himself in a threatening manner that was both unnerving and comical. His bloodshot eyes and occasional slurred speech belied the fact that he was no longer a figure to be reckoned with but instead a pompous drunk who spent his days lying in the lounger at his lakeside home, where he boasted of the largest and indisputably best-stocked bar on the lake.

Aunt Stella was faithful in her promise to keep him well-supplied with cases of Wild Turkey and Jack Daniels—so much so, in fact, that he eventually died of cirrhosis of the liver. As the years wore on and the liquor took its toll on his mind and body, he would occasionally sober up enough to drive downtown to the stockyards and sit in the lobby of the hotel that had been given to his wife many years before as a gift from some unknown Italian boyfriend. This was the very hotel in which my aunt had met him several years after she had sold it to an ambitious young entrepreneur who built an enormously popular steakhouse in one section of the downstairs and encouraged a local bank to build its offices in another section. A barbershop and my aunt's cigar stand completed the downstairs floor of the hotel.

A continuous stream of cowboys walked through the hotel lobby and out the swinging back doors to enter the Kansas City stockyards, which boasted of enormous pens of bellowing, odoriferous herds of cattle. My uncle had been one of those young cowboys who had caught my aunt's eye the first day he landed in Kansas City in the year 1925 to select bulls for a local rancher. His coal black hair and deep blue eyes prompted his friends to nickname him "The Black Irishman," and his quiet nature belied the fact that he had a powerful left hook that earned him the reputation of being as good in the boxing ring as he was at the poker tables. He was just the type of man that Aunt Stella had been looking for all of her life: handsome, quiet, loyal, and physically strong. The only problem with my uncle was his age.

He was ten years younger than her, but Aunt Stella's plans were not easily thwarted by mere numbers. She immediately started the legal process to have her birth date changed on her records to reflect that she was ten years younger and therefore young enough to date the unassuming young cowboy. As soon as she received her new records, she began courting him with a vengeance. His quiet nature had been a stumbling block to meeting women, so he never knew what hit him until after Stella had already tied the knot that bought him hook, line, and sinker.

She thought she was incredibly fortunate to have married this handsome young man who would let her have her way in spite of the fact that she would never be able to physically give him the family he longed for or a life in which he could claim her total loyalty. She was known throughout the Kansas City Bottoms as the lady who always got what she wanted because she would use any means to get whatever her heart desired. However, she grossly underestimated the determination of my uncle's strong will, and it was not until after they were married that she understood the scope of her husband's strength.

An incident took place in the first year of their marriage that changed Stella's attitude about who wore the pants in the family. After that time, Stella realized that not only was her new husband determined to be the head of his household, he would not be taken lightly as a source of strength and influence in all of the decisions they would make throughout the rest of their married life.

Life had not been easy for the couple because they were having to rent an upstairs room at Gus's and share a bathroom with three other boarders. Aunt Stella had been used to suitors treating her as a queen in return for sexual favors and witty humor, and she began to yearn for the excitement of her former life. Uncle Danny was not demonstrative in words or actions, so Aunt Stella had already grown bored with their marriage. Their plan to save for a house on the lake wasn't enough to keep Stella focused on their future together, and she became vulnerable to the striking young Italians who dropped by her cigar stand to joke and buy her expensive cigars.

Eventually, she succumbed to her lower nature when a former acquaintance dropped by her cigar stand on the way to the barbershop one afternoon, and she agreed to meet him later for an evening of dancing, dinner, and drinks at an exclusive bar on the Country Club Plaza. She made up a rather convincing story that she was going swimming with my mother and her sister at the local YWCA, which did not admit men on the premises. It seemed to be a foolproof plan. However, he wasn't so easily convinced that his wife was telling the truth because he hadn't been oblivious of her reputation in the months following their marriage. My uncle became suspicious when Stella wasn't home by 10:00 p.m. He knew that the other two women would not possibly stay at the YWCA that late, and he began to smell a rat. Gus watched him as he angrily threw on his shirt and pants and stomped down two flights of steps. In spite of her pleading for him to go back to bed and wait for his wife, he didn't say a word as he slammed the front door and jumped into his car.

Eventually, he found the bar at which my aunt and her friend were drinking, laughing, and swaying suggestively to the music of a black jazz band. He watched them from the shadows of the bar until he couldn't stand their gaiety any longer. At that point, he didn't say a word but surprised my aunt by knocking out her terrified friend with one swift blow and picking her up, kicking and screaming, all the way to the car. The police came after they had already left, and nobody knows what happened after that because when Aunt Stella came stumbling into the house, she had a bloody nose and bruises covering her arms.

As Dan pushed Stella up the stairs, Gus came flying out of her bedroom with her hair in its usual tight pin curls and her rumpled gown clinging to her ample body with the intentions of reprimanding her son-in-law. She was stopped in her tracks, however, as Danny shot her a glaring look that bordered on hate, and she immediately realized that this was not the time to confront the situation. She reluctantly backed into her bedroom with a grimace on her face and a knowing in her heart that this was one relationship she would not be free to meddle in without reaping dire consequences.

After that, my aunt was much more careful about the believability of her alibis because she was never caught again. That is not to say that she became a committed wife because her real nature was revealed through her advice to me, which was to secretly date an Italian on the side and I would keep a smile on my face just as she had done throughout her married life.

Gossip surrounded my aunt about the company she kept with the mob in the North Kansas City area, but nothing was ever known to be factual about these associations. However, she frequently kept a smile on her face when any one of them happened to come around to play poker in one of the hotel rooms or to bet on the electric horse racing game that was an ever-present feature. She and Danny made quite a colorful team of entrepreneurs, and Aunt Stella was a genius at making Uncle Danny think that he was the brains behind their ideas even though he continued to become more confused and less interested in business as liquor took over his thinking processes. I'm not sure when Danny developed his consuming thirst for alcohol, but I cannot remember any time when we were around him that he wasn't pouring a jigger of alcohol into his king-sized glass of choice. Danny and Stella's marriage lasted through the rest of their lives, but that was probably due to the fact that my uncle lived in a veil of drunkenness and didn't really care what happened as long as he had his case of expensive whiskey.

After living with my grandmother Gus for several

years, Aunt Stella and Uncle Danny finally saved up enough money to buy a small house on a residential lake on the outskirts of Kansas City. Everyone on the lake knew who my aunt and uncle were because they were constantly entertaining on the front lawn of their home. Dan would mow the grass in his bathing suit that hung precariously low under his enormously protruding stomach and occasionally would tan on the roof of their covered boat dock with nothing but a towel wrapped around his masculine parts. As the boats floated into the cove where they lived, most passengers waved and shouted a cheery hello to the O'Malleys. If there were no visitors on any given evening, Danny would motion the passengers to dock their boat and join him for a drink in his downstairs bar. He enjoyed sharing his hospitality and whiskey with others, but his most enjoyable times occurred when he donned his captain's hat and drove his speedboat around the lake. After crashing it against a buoy one foggy evening, however, he bought a party barge and took a varied assortment of noisy revelers out onto the lake nearly every afternoon. It was obvious that others stayed out of his way as he drunkenly maneuvered his floating beer joint in and out of the coves because the lake became strangely calm in the waters surrounding the errant party barge.

All of these perceived character flaws didn't seem to depress my uncle, however. Perhaps he felt that he had been forgiven of his sins because he and my aunt entertained the local priests and nuns by cooking them steaks on the grill and serving more expensive whiskey to them than he himself drank. He even carried a scar on his chest to attest to the fact that his loyalty was to the Catholic church in spite of the fact that it happened as a result of a drunken decision to pour gasoline on slow-burning coals that were lit to cook a meal for unexpected guests from the church rectory. Nonetheless, he had been taken by ambulance to the burn unit and experienced the thrill of being a hero to those who prayed the rosary over his healing body several times each day.

In spite of my uncle's deserved notorious reputation, not a Sunday went by that he wasn't sitting in the front pew of the local Catholic Church, listening intently to the homily being presented by one of his many priestly acquaintances. He generously gave his tithes to the church and ultimately had his name engraved on the back of one of the newest pews that had been acquired to help in the seating of a growing church population. His deceased mother had prayed for many years that Dan would become a Catholic priest, and perhaps he would have done just that if he hadn't had the misfortune of meeting my aunt at a hotel in the Kansas City Bottoms at an age when young men are driven by their own physical desires and fragile masculine egos.

Danny seemed to be Aunt Stella's anchor in her chaotic lifestyle, and she was determined to provide him with all the comforts he desired even though it included feeding his increasingly consuming addiction to alcohol. I wondered if he was secretly relieved that Grandmother Gus was finally gone and that maybe now his wife could spend time with him at the lake instead of spending most of her free time trying to gain her mother's love by carting her around town and ultimately stopping at our family's house so that we could share in her desire to make our grandmother comfortable. Nonetheless, Danny stoically sat staring at Grandmother Gus's lifeless body and seemed oblivious of the emotional turmoil that was creating havoc around him.

 I almost felt sorry for Uncle Danny because I knew how hard it was for us to be around Aunt Stella and her family for short periods of time, and his plight was much more long term in nature than ours. His presence at the lake softened Aunt Stella's hardened spirit, so we were always relieved to have him around even though he stayed in his downstairs bar during most of our visits. I must have been staring at him because he turned his face toward me and his lips formed a fleeting smile as though it were an accidental show of affection before he resumed his vigil beside the only one in the room who was willing to share their space with him—Candace's husband, the dentist.

Chapter Four

After my father made a show of reading all of the messages attached to the flowers, he again rose from his chair between my mother and the mysterious young lady and asked who sent the newly delivered spray of roses that had been placed by the casket as if they were an afterthought. I curiously glanced at him to see if he had been moved by the written message. Maybe he wasn't capable of showing emotion because his face took on the familiar stoic appearance that I had observed many times. My father, who was born to Susie Gustave and Frank Monroe Baxter on October 8, 1902, was the second son and the only one who bore any resemblance to his father. He was a small child with a bent toward mischievousness and hyperactivity, who adored his father in spite of the fact that he was seldom there to play with him or tuck him into bed.

It was Frank who convinced Gus to marry him after my father was born, despite her reputation for unofficially holding the keys to the city officials' hotel rooms. He wanted to seal their relationship after my father was born to give him a legitimate name and to prove to the town gossips that my father indeed was his. It was a tumultuous marriage and ended quite unexpectedly with him dying of strychnine poisoning about five years later.

After Gus bragged to several of her cronies that she had knocked off her bastard of a husband with rat poisoning, his family demanded that an official autopsy be undertaken. The autopsy revealed that there truly was a lethal amount of strychnine in his bloodstream, and Frank's family demanded that she be taken into custody immediately. The judge must have been one of Grandmother's bedmates because she only served a weekend in jail for her crime, and before she appeared in his court, the prosecutor was convinced that she gave the poison for medicinal reasons, as was the custom for those times in order to enhance sexual sensitivity and alleviate many of the side effects of bronchial infections.

Many years later, Patrick and our mother drove to the Rich Hill courthouse to search for a record of Gus's husband's death. A courthouse record keeper met him, and after he told her that he was looking for records implicating his grandmother of a murder that happened over eighty years before, she immediately said that records dating back that far were hardly ever kept. However, Patrick piqued her curiosity, and together they pulled out several volumes of ancient-looking records dating back to the year of the crime. The two sleuths were overjoyed and surprised to find the evidence they were looking for.

After making several copies of the records of Frank's

death, my brother and mother drove back to Kansas City, and Patrick sent the evidence to everyone in our family. Somehow, it gave him great satisfaction to uncover the ill-concealed crime which before that time seemed like a fictitious story that had been made up by those who didn't like my grandmother or were threatened by the life she represented. In his own way, he was making her accountable for at least one of the heinous crimes she had inflicted on another innocent person who had unwittingly stumbled across her path of destruction.

My father not only lost his father at this young and impressionable age but his mother as well because her newly acquired freedom didn't include a dedication to family cohesiveness. My grandfather Baxter's family vowed to make her pay for this crime against one of their own if she stayed in that area, but she continued to snub her nose at them by remaining long enough to remarry and move about Rich Hill as if nothing had happened at all. After a few months, however, her new husband's health began to be compromised by a heart condition that did not surface until after his marriage to Gus, and he talked her into moving to Kansas City to be closer to doctors who specialized in his form of heart disease. He agreed to take Maxine along with them but did not want the responsibility of the other three children, so Grandmother agreed and moved to Kansas City with her husband, Ed, and her youngest daughter, Maxine. The older siblings—Louis, Stella, and Victor—were unceremoniously dropped on their uncle's doorstep while their mother callously left them without any extra clothing or reparation for the food they would be eating out of their Uncle Clyde and Aunt Grace's already challenged food supply.

My father's family was not allowed to raise Victor because Gus refused to sign the papers to have him officially adopted by the Baxter clan, so at six years old, he was left to deal with the knowledge that his own mother didn't love him enough to demand that he be taken with her in spite of his stepfather's demands. It was another chance for Gus to make them pay for questioning her innocence in the death of their son. Another life was impacted negatively by my grandmother, who seemed to care less about any of her children.

My father never lost hope of living with his mother, however, and at sixteen years of age, he ran away from Appleton City and all of the bad memories that were part of his childhood. He drove through inclement weather as he fought to overcome the doubt that he felt about his mother's love for him and dreaded the reaction that he feared he might receive when she discovered him on her doorstep. He had gone without eating during his two-day journey in order to buy gasoline for his cycle and was weak with hunger when he finally stood in front of her door. He had not called to let her know he was coming, so she was completely shocked to open the door to the son she had left behind and who now stood in front of her as a teenage boy.

Her face revealed a lack of feelings for her son, and as he turned to leave, she reluctantly asked him in to eat supper with her and her ailing husband. His little sister didn't know that the young man who came into their kitchen was her big brother, and their mother did not care to introduce him as such. Gus nervously fed my father as the new man in her life sullenly stared at him across the table. After dinner, she told him that he couldn't stay there with them because the house wasn't big enough to accommodate another grown man. With a broken heart and no hope, my father contacted his father's youngest brother and found out that he was welcome to stay with him until he could find his own place to live.

His uncle Harry was a bachelor whose life was littered with the vices of those who had become bored with life in general and were not interested in any power beyond their own. He was well known to the local prostitutes and bookies as a generous customer and ruthless client. My father had not been acquainted with this form of lifestyle while living in Appleton City, so he was bombarded at an early age with a myriad of choices in which to express his most base desires in every way possible. This introduction to the shady activities of the city defined my father and impacted his life choices, which ultimately led to a general disregard for women and an intense abhorrence toward the permanency of married life. Furthermore, he fought against sexual addiction and an explosive temperament until cancer robbed him of his life at the age of eighty-six. Unfortunately, his love for music and a natural ability to see the humor in difficult situations weren't enough to elevate him to a place where he could overcome the imprints that were made on his life at an early age.

He and my mother, Ramona, were married for over fifty years, but there was no celebration honoring their anniversary. Instead, generalized cards were sent by members of the family acknowledging the fact that they had run a long race and endured incredible hardships along the way.

My father was a victim of Gus's refusal to take her parenting role responsibly, and as a result, a negative imprint was left on the rest of his life as well as on the lives of his wife and three children. His attempts at fatherhood were inconsistent and mechanical even though he had times where his humor brought us all together in raucous bouts of laughter.

My father had many strange ideas on how to conduct himself in the realm of fatherhood. He could be incredibly mean and dangerously on the edge one minute and insanely humorous the next. I was not impacted as deeply by his mood swings as my brothers were, however, because he was particularly combative with them. This is not to say that I wasn't scared of his anger, but I don't think I was on the receiving end of his general disdain for humanity as often as they were. My older brother was the recipient of a lion's share of his physical and verbal abuse, and as I look back now, I think I know the reasons behind my father's unreasonable treatment of Patrick.

To begin with, my brother was talented beyond any level that my father could ever hope to attain in all areas of the creative arts. He could play the piano like a virtuoso at the age of ten and had a voice that was pitch-perfect. He was proficient in most all artistic medias and excelled in the performing arts. He even secured a cameo appearance in a fairly popular movie that was produced by one of his good friends.

My father might have also suspected that his eldest son exhibited certain homosexual traits even though he dated girls off and on throughout his high school and early adult years. Dad had a general distrust of anything he could not explain in his own mind, and he would not take any credit for his responsibility in any situation that could point out his incompetence. If he even suspected that his relationship with his eldest son was a contributing factor to Patrick's homosexuality, my father would have never admitted it to himself or anyone else. I remember one incident in which most children would have been traumatized forever, and I'm not sure that Patrick wasn't.

Our relatives had driven from California and dropped by to stay the night with us before continuing their journey to Springfield, where much of their family continued to live. My father became extremely nervous when anyone besides our immediate family came to visit because he had absolutely no social skills and resented sharing his groceries with that many other people. He apparently forgot the many times that our family stayed for a week at a time with them when we traveled to California after his many disputes with the boss at the machine shop where he happened to be working at the time.

He paced the floor behind my mother the night before their arrival as she prepared food ahead of time so that she might have the next day free to visit with her sister and the rest of her family. My father became so upset over the amount of food that she was preparing that he threatened to give her half of what they usually spent on the next week's groceries and throw the pan of brisket out in the yard to show his displeasure. Finally, my mother turned and faced him with a steely resolve and called his bluff about the next week's grocery budget by reminding him that his palate would suffer along with the rest of the family's if he cut her short. He turned and stomped out of the kitchen with a warning that she would be sorry about her insensitivity toward him, and sure enough, he made her pay the next day by an incredible act of cruelty toward Patrick.

My mother's sister and her family were due to arrive around noon the following day, and Mother was busy finishing up in the kitchen. Dad was sullenly reading the paper in the living room while we three children played outside with our frisky Spitz dog, Zippy. Patrick had filled a large tin can with water for the dog to drink from and had just turned to wave as our relatives drove onto our driveway. Just as he started to run toward the car, the heel of his bare right foot came down upon the jagged edge of the can, slicing it to the bone.

My father yelled for him to come welcome his cousins as he doubled over in pain from the wound. After my father yelled the second time without any response from my brother, who had been rendered speechless from seeing so much blood, Dad ran across the yard and tore my brother's shirt completely off of him for not answering when he was called. It was then that he noticed the blood that was covering my brother's foot and in his embarrassment shoved Patrick into the house to have my mother clean and medicate his gaping wound. He had been successful in ruining another joyful moment for everyone in our family and seemed to be smugly proud of himself for making our California relatives less than comfortable later when they sat down to eat my mother's delicious meal.

After we ate and our mother sat down to visit with

her sister, all of us cousins ran and played in the yard until the sun began to set. We were looking forward to staying up late in our attic bedroom and visiting until we fell asleep from exhaustion, but for whatever the reason, my aunt's husband announced that they needed to be getting down the road before it got any later. My uncle stood up to shake my father's hand before he rounded up his family to resume their trip, and to all of our dismay, they left almost as soon as they had arrived. My mother was completely saddened by their sudden departure and cleaned up the supper dishes with tears of anger and frustration brimming in her eyes. Patrick's foot healed after several weeks of my mother's expert medical attention, but my father had added another wedge in their marriage and in his relationship with his eldest son.

My older brother wasn't always the only one who found himself to be at the wrong place at the wrong time when it came to Dad's anger. An episode that happened during one of our mother's prolonged stays at the hospital stands out in my mind because it inadvertently involved our elderly neighbors as well as my younger brother, Michael, and me. Mother had been taken by ambulance earlier that day because the doctor couldn't calm her escalating heartbeat, and he was afraid that she would die quickly if she didn't receive expert medical attention. After she left, my father announced that we were to make ourselves a sandwich and be in the house before it became dusk.

Our older brother was playing his records and lying on his bed upstairs while Michael and I sat on the divan, frightened by the quietness of the downstairs. We both agreed that a bicycle ride would be just what the doctor might order to calm our fears and proceeded to fly out of our yard and onto the street in our search to erase the reality of our situation. We were enjoying the fluttering of the playing cards that we had attached to our spokes and whizzed up and down our street until it was too dark to see anything but the lights in the windows of our neighbors' houses. All of a sudden, Michael and I remembered our father's warning and, with the adrenaline rushing through our bodies, raced each other to try to get to the house before he returned home from the hospital. Both of our hearts fell when we saw his car parked in the garage, and we knew our fate was sealed.

It didn't seem quite as important to reach our destination in a timely fashion, so we both got off of our bikes and pushed them into the garage beyond our father's still-warm car. We opened the back door as quietly as we could, hoping our father had fallen asleep in his chair, but no such luck. As soon as he saw us coming in the door, he rushed toward us with the fire from hell burning in his eyes, and we both reacted at the same time by doing something we had never done before—we turned and ran away from him as fast as our legs could go.

During his pursuit of us, he picked up a board from the side of the house and threateningly held it above his head as he sprinted after us, closing ground with every passing second. My life passed before my eyes as I felt him getting nearer, and I began to wet my pants as I felt his hand grab the back of my neck while he positioned my body to receive my punishment. My brother stopped when he saw that I had been caught and readied himself for his punishment as well. Just as my father raised the board above his head for my first lick, the neighbor next door shouted to my father asking if there was anything wrong. I know that he and his wife had been observing our saga through their dining room window and were alarmed by the fury that our father was focusing on us kids. The streetlight in front of our house lit up our death-defying race, and after our second time around, our neighbor must have fairly ran out of his house and down his front stairs to intervene in the escalating situation.

Mr. Jones did what he thought was right; and even though he wasn't sure what the outcome might be, he came to our aid by diverting my father's attention. After talking to Dad for a few minutes, Mr. Jones asked if he and his wife could feed my little brother and I supper while my father relaxed. Reluctantly, my father agreed to let Michael and I eat with the Joneses with a warning for us to expect our punishment later. After an hour of visiting with our neighbors and eating a delicious, home-cooked meal, we returned home ready to accept any discipline our father had to offer. However, the house was dark, and Michael and I were able to slip into bed without having to face our punishment that night. The next day, our father seemed to forget his promise to discipline us, and we never spoke of the incident again.

As we grew older, our punishments became more caustic, which created an inward rebellion in each of us siblings. Dad was a reactive person by nature and never stopped to find out the circumstances behind any of our questionable situations. Therefore, we were punished as the guilty party regardless of the fact that we might have been the innocent victims of the crime in question. One such incident happened during my eleventh year when I had reached puberty, much to my chagrin.

We all shared one bathroom in our two-story house, and that posed a problem for a young girl such as me who found it completely embarrassing to share any details of my impending maturity with anyone in my household for various personal reasons. On the particular day of the incident that deepened my already consuming fear of my father, I had slept later than usual before jumping out of bed and getting ready for school. Dad usually was gone by the time my brothers fought over who would occupy the bathroom before class, but on this day, he stood before the mirror in his baggy shorts with shaving cream covering his face.

It was imperative that I use the restroom and freshen up before I ran out of the front door to start my two-mile trek to school. My heart pounded as if it would jump out of my chest as I politely asked him to leave the bathroom while I used the toilet. He didn't miss a stroke as he indignantly told me to use the bathroom while he continued to shave or go outside in the bushes if I didn't like the situation. In my anger and repulsion over his demand, I raised my voice and asked him to leave the bathroom before I called my mother to rectify the situation. At that moment, he reacted in the same way that he might have when attacked by a rabid animal and began to hit at me with his hand that held the razor.

An unbelievable terror gripped me as I raised my arms

over my head to protect my face against his onslaught of blows, and before he was brought back to his senses by my shrill screams, both of my arms were dripping with blood from an innumerable amount of superficial cuts that covered the area from my elbows to the wrists of both arms. By the time my mother appeared at the door with her face paling from the shock of what she saw before her, my father had composed himself enough to blame the incident on my snotty mouth. My father could see that his excuse was falling on deaf ears, so he abruptly rinsed the shaving cream off of his face before he pushed Mother aside and stomped into their bedroom, where he proceeded to get dressed.

    I found out later that this was his first day at another machine shop where he had worked twice before and was rehired for his craftsmanship in return for his promise to keep his explosive temper under control. Mother didn't make me attend school that day, and together, we tried to come up with a story that we could tell my classmates and teacher if they questioned me about the cuts on my arms. We knew that it would do no good to shame my father about his actions, so we chalked up the incident as another conduct malfunction and determinedly set our minds to focus on our blessings instead of the pain in our lives.

    My father was quirky, angry, and many times unpredictable, but he was also unafraid to confront most situations that would have possibly gone unnoticed by anyone else whose thoughts were trained on more normal daily activities. He made several citizen's arrests against drunken drivers and caught a multitude of trash-throwing marauders, taking them completely by surprise with his bellowing accusations. One particularly humorous confrontation took place when he and my mother were in line behind a very overweight woman whose car was next in line to conduct her business at the local drive-through bank window.

My father had commented on the fact that the reason she was so fat was because of the huge bag of fast food that she was stuffing down her throat. It was hard for my father to wait any length of time for anyone, so his patience was already being challenged by the slow-moving bank employee, and he began to focus on the fast food junkie ahead of him. Mother momentarily rested her head back against the seat as she shut out the demands of the day and was abruptly startled by my father's explosive exit from the car. She couldn't believe her eyes when she saw Dad knock on the window of the heavy lady's car and demand that she pick up the empty food bag that she had carelessly thrown onto the pavement in front of the headlights of his car.

At first, the lady pretended not to notice his persistent knocking on her window but soon relented when he threatened to tell the bank president about her disregard for the cleanliness of his grounds. She gingerly opened her window just wide enough to let my father push the trash through and make a rude suggestion on how she could lose those unwanted pounds. She shouted out that he was a crazy man and drove on by the window without ever stopping to finish her banking business. My mother had a keen sense of humor, so she wasn't completely taken aback by the situation. Instead, she silently prayed that the young lady hadn't been completely traumatized by her encounter with my dad and wondered how many more of these situations she would have to endure in their marriage.

Whenever my father felt the urging to change his surroundings by trekking across country to visit my mother's two youngest sisters and their families, he usually didn't give us much time to think about the ordeal that we would have to face. Our household became a beehive of activity as each one of us made quick decisions about what to take on our unplanned trip. We usually had a pet or two that had to be cared for during our absence, so my father called Grandmother Gus with a request to have her babysit with the animals that couldn't be cared for by our neighbors. Her rather large backyard seemed to be the ideal place for our pets to stay while we were gone, but we usually didn't see them again after they were unceremoniously dumped off on our way to California. We figured that Grandmother Gus probably got tired of feeding them after the first day or two and left the gate open so they could experience the freedom of the open road. I sensed my father's relief when we left his mother's house and hoped that his sense of peace would last throughout the trip. However, this was never the case because it didn't take long for one of us to irritate him, and the tone of the rest of the excursion was set.

Our vacations were nothing less than endurance trials that took an incredible toll on the whole family. They were usually unplanned and took place as the result of my father's frequent, uncontrollable temper tantrums that resulted in him being dismissed from his job assignments.

I suspect that his unhappiness with his jobs was the result of an abhorrence to monotony, and it seemed that a change of scenery was the only prescription for this problem. He would usually be informed by noon that he no longer had a job, so he would immediately call my mother to tell her that we would be leaving for California as soon as he came home from work that same afternoon. My mother was thrilled to be able to visit with her sisters and their families, so she fried chicken and packed enough other food to carry us through the entire trip. My father never paid to eat in a restaurant, so we either ate out of our stash of cold food or he cooked potatoes, along with bacon and eggs, over an open fire on the side of the road.

I often wonder what the passing motorists thought when they observed our family of five picnicking together as if we were happily enjoying every moment of our vacation. Little did they know that we were all pushing our physical and psychological well-being to the limit, and with each passing moment, our determination to survive until we arrived at our destination was wearing unbelievably thin.

First of all, we three siblings were embarrassed beyond imagination to be in plain sight of the passing motorists as we obediently swallowed down the crude staples that my father cooked in his oversized iron skillet and shoved at each of us while shooting us a look that emphasized the fact that we had better not say one negative word about what he had prepared. Mother looked on in dismay when she saw the discouragement in our demeanor as we each took our plate of food to our own shady respite and turned our backs to the gawking travelers while swallowing down our meal with great gulps of water. We couldn't wait to eat the delicious tacos and chocolate cake that my aunts always had prepared for our visits, but we knew that eating our father's food was a reality that had to be dealt with at the moment, and our dream of better times would take place in just a few more hours.

Sometimes, those roadside eating excursions took on an adventurous bent when my father spied an interesting outcropping of rock near a riverbed or a flat place beside a mountain stream. It was then that our usual bill of fare took on a new dimension while we were allowed to inspect our surroundings with the curiosity that God only allows children to possess. Gigantic, hairy tarantulas lurked under multicolored boulders, and beautiful wildflowers grew in profusion on the banks of the streams. Smooth rocks worn into great, round stepping-stones provided a path for us to cross the clear, freezing mountain streams, and rainbow-colored lizards scuttled away from our inquiring eyes. These were truly the moments that nearly made up for the other agonizing aspects of our journeys, and I have tried to concentrate on them instead of dwelling on the negatives of our Route 66 sagas.

I will never forget the newfangled round water cooler that hung like a cylindrical bomb on the passengers' window of our front door. Always before, we who sat in the backseat had to slather Vaseline on our lips to ward off a serious case of cracked lips from the oven-like hot air that blew relentlessly on us from all four open windows. It did not occur to our father that he could have alleviated some of our misery by merely letting us roll our windows up halfway instead of making us withstand the brunt of a sixty-mile-an-hour wind for two straight days.

We all watched in hopeful anticipation of a cool backseat as my father wrestled with the cumbersome apparatus that promised us sheer comfort on our way to the West Coast. Our expectations were short-lived, however, because not only did the new cooler do little to alleviate our situation, it constantly leaked onto the person who sat on the passenger side of both the front and backseat. The right shoulder of my mother became completely soaked from the constant dripping until she took over the responsibility of driving, and whoever sat directly behind it in the backseat didn't have to wash their face that night because they were cleaner than they had been in months from the unending bombardment of drenching spray.

My father couldn't stay awake for more than an hour at a time, so it became his turn to ride shotgun much sooner than the rest of us had hoped. We were all curious to see how he would handle the relentless shower of lukewarm water. We were all disappointed that he didn't pitch the cooler onto the side of the road. Instead, he traded places with whoever was sitting directly behind the driver and immediately fell asleep while the rest of us continued to suffer from the leaking monster that seemed destined to be a part of our family excursions from then on. When we finally arrived in sunny California, I had a sore throat, and my brothers had both developed a rather deep cough, but we were so grateful to escape our transportation from hell that we tumbled out of the car nearly before it came to a complete stop. My brothers and I silently thanked God that the sun was shining so that our clothes would soon be dry and we could enjoy our visit in paradise for the next several days.

My mother was a good driver, but even the best of drivers have to rest occasionally before reaching their destination. Even when both of her arms were in casts from an accident that occurred while visiting the excavation site of our new home, she still drove at least eight hours a day without complaining. It was usually late at night when my father relented and pulled over at the first motel that sported a vacancy sign and the appearance of being within his budget. Most people who were concerned about the welfare of their family wouldn't have parked in front of those seedy-looking inns long enough to fix a flat tire. My father wasn't into comfort or safety, so we ended up staying in some of the dirtiest, oldest, and cheapest motels along the road.

I remember my younger brother crying after we carried our luggage into one of these rooms because he didn't want to turn out the lights. There were so many bugs running under the bed that he was afraid to put his feet on the floor, and my mattress smelled so rank that I slept on top of the spread while burying my nose into the pillow until I felt like I was suffocating. It seemed like hours before we all fell asleep, and before the sun could color the eastern sky, my father was up and ready to start the next day's journey in spite of the fact that my mother hadn't gotten enough rest to drive safely. We warily stumbled out of bed and headed back to our waiting chariot without uttering a word because there were no words that could have possibly been passed between us that would have adequately expressed our utter contempt for the situation.

Another overnight adventure turned out to be more pleasant than we had anticipated, even though I have often wondered why we seemed to be the only visitors who had paid to stay the night. We were in the mountains when a thick fog completely blocked out everything within a few inches of our headlights, and both my mother and father agreed that it was foolish to put ourselves in danger if we didn't have to. No sooner was the decision to stop for the night agreed upon than a great lodge appeared on the side of the road. There were absolutely no other cars in sight, but we chalked that up to the fact that we were probably the only ones crazy enough to venture out in such a thick blanket of fog. Maybe it was because my brothers and I had seen too many scary movies at the Englewood Theater, but the whole situation didn't sit quite right with any of us.

My father told us to sit tight while he went in to haggle over the price of our room as the rest of us quietly sat and watched wide-eyed as the swirling fingers of fog seemed to clutch at our car. After what seemed like a lifetime of waiting, Dad fairly skipped out to the car and informed us that the owner had rented us two rooms for less money than he normally charged for a single-bed accommodation. He had planned to be at full capacity, but the fog had taken away all of his customers except for us, and he was willing to take less because he feared for our safety.

The downstairs was an enormous eating hall furnished with at least ten harvest tables topped with kerosene lanterns and checkered tablecloths. A gigantic moose head looked down from one end of the hall, while an assortment of stuffed wildlife stood on shelves situated at different levels on the other end. I had read about Earnest Hemingway and his grand collection of stuffed animals and wondered if he had taken a side trip to the western part of the United States before moving on to grander expeditions.

The owner, a tiny, bald-headed man who seemed to find it hard to move, brought my thoughts back to the present as he led us up a stairway that had been built close enough to the stuffed moose head that one could reach out and touch his fur. I was so taken aback by his enormous staring eyeball that I couldn't wait to shut the door to my room and dream about what adventures tomorrow might bring. Each room opened upon a walkway that completely surrounded the great eating area, and a wooden railing separated us from becoming airborne if we forgot to watch our steps.

Mom and Dad shared one room, and my brothers and I shared the other. There were bunk beds on one side of the room and a massive, natural pine bed on the other end. It felt as though we were invading the bunkhouse of a cattle baron, and I could almost imagine the cowboys coming in to rest after a roundup on the trail. Red and beige plaid cotton curtains and matching bedspreads created a pleasant contrast with the rough pine furniture and imitation kerosene lamps that sat on the nightstands beside each bed.

As usual, my older brother claimed the large bed, and Michael and I were left to quibble over which bunk bed we wanted to sleep in. He wanted the top bunk, and that was okay by me because I didn't want to be that close to the ceiling in case a spider decided to drop down and take up residence with whoever invaded his space. We had to share our bathroom, and as usual, Patrick jumped in ahead of us. By the time he reappeared, Michael was already asleep, and I was livid with anger at his complete disregard for our comfort. I pushed him aside as he wrapped all three bath-sized towels around his squeaky-clean body and locked the door behind me. It didn't take me long, however, to realize that he had used all of the large towels, and the only ones left were the hand-sized towels that would barely dry both my hair and the rest of my body, let alone Michael's.

Something broke inside of me, and I threw open the door with clenched jaw and a determination to make him pay for his self-centeredness. We had all been through hell, and each of us deserved to experience some level of comfort without having to beg for our just due. I forgot that I was no match for Patrick physically and proceeded to run as fast as my ten-year-old legs could go straight toward my startled brother, who resembled a Roman statesman with the fluffy white towels wrapped loosely around his pudgy middle. He threw his hands up to stop the hurtling mass of bony arms and legs that was bearing down upon his middle section, and his towels fell to the floor, leaving him completely exposed. I was not impressed by his less-than-perfect physique and fell on the floor laughing at the absurdity of the situation while he scrambled to cover his body with the plaid bedspread.

I knew he would not tell on me because he would have to admit how selfish he had been, and he knew that our father wouldn't cut either of us any slack. I took two of his towels and hung them up for Michael to use the next morning while I used the hand towels that were hanging on the silver rack behind the stool. Patrick had fallen asleep before I finished using the shower, so the situation didn't escalate any further, and we all settled down for a good night's sleep.

I was awakened by the sound of running water, and when I tiptoed over to look out of the window, I was pleasantly surprised to see a gurgling mountain stream running beside the lodge. The morning sun was dancing over the churning waves, sending a million flecks of light hurtling back up into the atmosphere, making me feel that God was doing something special just for me. At that moment, I forgot all of the negatives that seemed to accompany our family outings and quietly celebrated my oneness with nature.

I pulled my jeans up and threw on my shirt and red sandals hoping to tiptoe outside before anyone else woke up, but my father was already dressed and sitting at one of the tables eating a breakfast complete with steak, eggs, and a large mug of coffee. I'm sure that I startled him because he immediately began to eat his food at an alarming rate as he glanced furtively toward the rooms in which the rest of our family was sleeping. With irritation creeping into his voice, he asked why I had gotten up so early and where I planned to go without telling anyone else in the family what my plans were. I told him about the beautiful stream I had seen outside of my window and that I was going to put my feet in the rushing water before either one of my brothers could ruin my oneness with nature. A smile tugged at the corner of his lips as the same little man who showed us to our rooms the night before asked me if I wanted anything to eat.

Before my father could deny my request for a hot meal, the little man declared that breakfast came with the price of the room, and I was soon devouring my own fare of scrambled eggs, bacon, and buttered toast. Afterward, my father and I climbed down to the beautiful little stream and silently watched as the mountain gave up its icy water to flow over the rounded rocks and disappear around the gigantic boulders that lined the canyon wall. We sat there quietly for what seemed to be an eternity before my father announced that it was time to start on our journey home. I vowed to myself that someday I would return and stay a week on this beautiful mountain, but I have not done it yet and am not sure that I could find it again.

When Dad and I walked into the lodge, my mother and two brothers had just finished their breakfast and curiously asked where Dad and I had been. As if he wanted to keep our adventure a secret between us, he ignored their questions and declared that it was time to get our things ready to get on the road once again. Both Patrick and Michael stared at me with questioning eyes, but I didn't reveal my whereabouts and climbed the stairs to pack my belongings for the trip back to Missouri. I never told either of my brothers about that glorious mountain stream and to this day occasionally wake up with the memory of that display of nature running through my mind as though it happened just last week.

The viewing was lasting much longer than my brothers and I had anticipated, and I could tell that I wasn't the only one who was ready to get back to the house. Dad looked tired as he shifted in his seat, and I wondered how much longer he could sit still before calling it a night. I made a mental note to ask him if he remembered that day on the mountain when we shared that beautiful sight of the sun shining in the mountain stream, but the time for reminiscing never seemed to present itself, and I left Kansas City at the end of my visit without ever bringing up our well-kept secret.

The funeral director had come to the door of our viewing room several times to see if our family was still there and seemed to be disappointed that we had not moved from our chairs. We all wondered how much longer Aunt Stella would stand staring at her mother before she called it an evening and signal to the rest of the group that we could all depart.

Chapter Five

After watching the intermittent stream of visitors at the viewing, my attention was drawn to Mother as she sat in her rightful position beside my father. I noticed her occasional sideways glance at the brazen trollop who obviously was unaware of the rules of social etiquette and observed the determined set of her delicate jaw. Mother had long ago relinquished her dream of having a committed husband, so it was obvious in her demeanor that this situation was nothing more than another bump in the road of her marriage.

Her story began without the usual fanfare of babies born to the more affluent families in the city. It was a snowy night on November 28, 1910, when Ramona Malinda Polk was born to Emmett Jefferson and Martha Ellen Polk. The blizzard-like conditions blew a relentless blast of frigid air against the ill-fitting windowpanes of their frame farmhouse that sat on a small tract of land outside of Springfield, Missouri.

Ellen had been in relentless pain throughout her labor

and was suffering in their four-poster, hand-hewn bed with only the widow on the adjacent farm present to lend a helping hand. Jeff had driven their wagon to Springfield to pick up the midwife, and as the storm increased in intensity, the horses began to slow down and resist his grip on the reins. Suddenly, the light from the midwife's window spilled out onto the snow, and she ran out of her front door carrying a rather large valise filled with supplies to deliver babies that were born to the farm families surrounding the city.

Word had spread that Mrs. Polk was about to deliver, and she had been prepared all afternoon to accompany the person who would drive her to deliver the fourth Polk child. The storm had become increasingly intense throughout the afternoon, and she began to doubt that Ellen would have anyone besides Jeff to help her deliver the new baby and wondered why nobody had shown up. She wondered if Mr. Polk had delayed too long at the widow's farm in order to make sure her livestock had been sufficiently watered and fed. Wagging tongues had spread a rumor that Jeff and the widow were spending more and more time together as Ellen's pregnancy had progressed. Her thoughts were interrupted when she heard the whinny of an oncoming team of horses, and she shook off any of the negative feelings she had been harboring against Jeff Polk in order to focus on the job that lay ahead of her.

A sigh of relief turned into fear as Jeff drove his team of horses into the blinding snow. Enormous mounds of snow began to pile up on both sides of the road, and it became increasingly more difficult to determine the direction of their journey. Their situation became more dangerous by the minute until Jeff decided that it was foolish to push onward into the night. Just as he started to turn the team around to follow the ruts in the road back to the midwife's house, Jeff recognized the Polk fence. The wire barrier that had been erected to protect their land from animal predators served as a beacon to lead the snowy travelers to their destination.

Their wagon rumbled and creaked up the road to the front door of the impeccably cared for farmhouse and barn. The aging but rather agile midwife jumped off of the wagon even before Jeff had brought the horses to a complete standstill. The older children had been listening expectantly at the front door for the sound of familiar horses' hooves and threw it open even before the wagon had been brought to a complete stop. A cheery fire crackled in the open fireplace as the three Polk children took up their vigil on the horsehair couch. An oval rag rug that had been skillfully designed and braided to cover the gleaming hardwood floors lay under their feet.

Bonnie, the oldest and most responsible, had followed her mother's instructions earlier that day and had made a cherry pie out of the dried fruit from their spring crop. Nellie, the widow from the farm next door, stood savoring a large piece of the pie as she warmed herself near the hearth. Occasionally, she paced the floor while putting as much distance between the suffering woman and herself as she could.

Jeff took a position near the bed with an indifferent attitude that exposed his annoyance with Ellen for controlling his time with her ongoing labor. He had promised Nell, the widow, that he would take her home after the baby arrived, and he was anxious to leave. His wife's painful screams had unnerved him, and he felt somewhat responsible for her discomfort, but not enough to hold her hand in his as she responded to the midwife's instructions to push at the onset of each contraction.

Nell walked to the bedroom door and glanced at Jeff's face to determine what feelings he might be having for his wife. She smugly glanced away after she realized that Jeff appeared almost indifferent to the drama that was unfolding before him. The midwife held back her anger and concentrated on the job that lay ahead. Her patient clutched the family Bible and pushed with all of the strength that she had left. Suddenly, a blond and dimpled baby girl was born amid the confusion of orders being shouted by the midwife to bring clean white cloths and the lusty screams of the newest addition to the growing Polk family. The midwife overlooked the suggestive glances that Mr. Polk and his neighbor were throwing at each other and worked to make her patient as comfortable as possible.

The older children were sent to bed in the loft, and the midwife settled down on a feather bed that was placed on the floor near Ellen so that she could tend to her needs throughout the night. Jeff excused himself to take his neighbor home and thanked the midwife for coming out on such a wintry evening. As the sun rose the next morning, sending sparkling paths across the newly fallen snow, Jeff returned to his wife and new baby daughter as if there was nothing wrong with his actions. The midwife placed the tools of her trade into her satchel and announced to Jeff that she was ready to return to her own home. Without a word, he turned around and helped her up into the wagon that would return her to her cottage and away from the hypocrisy that surrounded the head of the Polk family.

The midwife visited the Polk farm three more times before the last child was born, but Mr. Polk did not become any more committed to his family after their number swelled to nine. Martha Ellen was a beautiful woman, with piercing blue eyes and raven black hair that hung to her waist. Her long, thin legs and graceful hands stimulated her husband's desire for her, but his heart belonged to the widow next door who came to their house every morning and tauntingly shaved Jeff's beard as Ellen tended to the children and pretended not to care. Jeff asked for a divorce on many occasions, but his wife refused to give him one because he was the father of their children, and she believed it was a sin to divorce. He lived at both farms for several years and became increasingly more irritable and surly whenever he was at home.

Ellen was an expert cook and seamstress and could garden circles around anyone else in the county. Her sons helped her plant and harvest vegetables and fruit that won blue ribbons each year at the county fair, and she became a pillar of the Church of God, where she raised her children to fear God and abide by the words of the Bible.

Her sons grew to be remarkably handsome, combining the best characteristics from both their father and mother. When they rode into town on the backs of their spirited horses, their black, curly hair and blue eyes turned the heads of the available young ladies in Springfield. Jeff didn't give them much time to court the young lasses, however, because they were responsible for all of the chores on their farm while he tended to the farm next door. They were severely disciplined, and when they weren't attending church, they had to study and help their mother chop wood and take care of the smaller children. Ellen tried to soften their otherwise bleak existence by rewarding them with a spotless house, delicious meals, and an incredible love that was driven by her desire to please the Lord.

Ramona and her sisters were also kept busy by the constant demands of a family who lived before modern appliances could make housekeeping an art instead of drudgery. They washed their clothes and curtains in large vats of hot water and lye soap on Mondays. On Tuesdays, they ironed curtains, sheets, pillowcases, and their father's white shirts that had been meticulously starched and bleached. All of the children took turns weeding the garden and washing dishes after each meal. Quilts were batted outside on the clothesline, and pies had to be cooked and placed in the pie safe in preparation for the after-church visitors who came to their house each Sunday afternoon.

The memory of the week's hard work seemed to pale as the visitors spilled through the front door. It was a tradition that anyone who wished to eat with the Polks on Sunday was welcome to come and sit around the enormous harvest table and be a part of the hospitality that was joyfully shared along with generous portions of the Scripture. White, starched curtains gently ruffled in the breeze while the scent of fruit blossoms or the perfume of seasonal flowers floated through the windows of the scrubbed and pleasant farmhouse. Initially, it was embarrassing for Ellen to entertain guests without her husband being present, but as the years wore on, there was an unspoken understanding between friends and family that the Polks were married in name only and that his loyalties did not lie with his wife or children.

Ramona drew the brunt of her father's disapproval because she was a sickly child who demanded more of his wife's time and concern than he was willing to graciously share during his short visits to the house. Her blond, curly hair and enormous green eyes seemed to appear whenever he occasionally felt the urge to lie with his wife. He slept in their bed so infrequently throughout my mother's childhood years that it became her habit to crawl into bed with Ellen whenever a storm threatened to break or when the frequent fevers racked her fragile body.

Jeff wasn't receptive to having any of the children sleeping with him, so whenever Ramona tried to crawl into the safety of their bed, he would kick her onto the floor and tell her to go to her own bed as she sobbed in confusion and fear. Her older sister, Bonnie, would whisper to her at the bedroom door, convincing her to come to bed with her while Jeff would pull Ellen's flannel robe up to her waist and enjoy his wife's body as she cried silent tears of anger and resentment for what their marriage had become. Jeff's infrequent visits to his marriage bed were a sad reminder of the wife and family he had neglected for so many years, so his visits never lasted longer than the time it took for him to leave a pall on the household before he disappeared again for weeks at a time. He also had to face the fact that his family was getting along quite well without his presence and seemed happier when he wasn't there.

It wasn't until the last Polk child was left at home and his health began to fail that Jeff finally became a full-time father and husband. Nell, the widow, finally grew tired of waiting for him to marry her and accepted the proposal of a prosperous widower from the next county. She sold her farm and left without a formal farewell, and none of the Polk family ever saw her again.

My mother turned fourteen in the year 1924 and had grown weary with the constant grind of farm life and the strict upbringing by her mother and father. She was by far the most beautiful of the Polk girls, even though they all were attractive in their own ways. Her blond hair set her apart from the rest of them, and the boys came from other farms to try their luck at courting her. Ellen would let them stay long enough to visit on the front porch and have a fresh piece of pie or a handful of cookies, but whenever they saw Mr. Polk, they would excuse themselves and leave before he could usher them off of his land. His nickname was Old White Collar because Ellen starched his shirt collars to accommodate his desire to look well-dressed and successful, but the young men who used the term saw him as an overbearing, threatening oaf of a man who made everyone's lives around him miserable.

That spring after school let out for the summer months, Ramona was invited to stay in Kansas City with her older brother and sister until school started in the fall. Ellen knew that Jeff would make Ramona's life miserable with his constant harping and unhappiness about her attitude toward the farm, so she reluctantly allowed her to leave. Ramona's heart broke as she looked out of the train window and saw the tears flowing down her mother's face. Ellen suspected that her beautiful daughter would never return to live on the Polk farm again, and she was right. That was the beginning of a new life for her fourth child, and from then on, the only time Ramona went back to Springfield was to visit.

Poor health and an innocence of the realities of life did not deter Ramona from jumping into her new dream of a life beyond the rigors of the farm and the suffocating restrictions of a legalistic mother and joyless father. The older boys had already left the farm and were leading their own lives where they felt they had some control over their own situations. The only children who were left on the farm were the two youngest girls and their baby brother. Ramona was especially close to her twelve-year-old sister, Edna, and hated to leave her but did not want to miss a chance to get away from the farm for the next several months.

Ramona arrived at the Kansas City train terminal early on the evening of June 3, 1924, in the middle of a torrential downpour of rain. Lightning and high winds had threatened to delay the train at a depot outside of Kansas City, but the engineer decided that the worst part of the storm had already gone past and they would proceed on schedule to their destination. Ramona stared at the enormously overpowering skyline as the train snaked into the huge terminal, and she suddenly felt small and alone. Her homemade clothes and well-worn shoes seemed to scream out the fact that she was just a simple country girl who did not fit in with anyone around her. She forgot her self-consciousness, however, as soon as the train entered the terminal and noisily slowed down to a complete stop.

Brakes ground and steam hissed as Ramona strained to see out her rain-streaked window. A wave of fear clutched at her heart as she began to worry if the storm might have delayed her brother and sister from picking her up. Her knees began to shake, and her heart started beating in that irregular cadence that was usually accompanied with lightheadedness and dizzy spells. A young man who was sitting on the seat across from Ramona noticed that she was under duress, so he offered to take her suitcase down from the bin above her head. That brought her back to reality, and after thanking him profusely, she stepped down onto the waiting platform.

The bustling terminal teemed with a myriad of sights and sounds. People of all ages and appearances seemed to be knit together in a single desire to reach their particular destination. Crying babies, newspaper hawkers, and the clicking of an army of feet on the marble tiles began to engulf her in an avalanche of noise. The pungent smells from a countless number of concession stands mingled with the thick fragrances of perfume that had been generously applied to conceal perspiration odors on the bodies of travelers under pressure to meet their various timetables. As Ramona's nerves reacted to the barrage on her senses, her heart again began beating erratically, and those familiar black spots danced before her eyes.

The conductor who had helped Ramona exit the train noticed she wasn't feeling well and took her arm as he led her to a nearby bench. After bringing her a cold glass of water and making sure that she had gotten past her fainting spell, he left her to return to his responsibilities on the waiting train. As she swallowed down feelings of hysteria and doubt, the crowd seemed to part, and there, directly in front of the bench, stood her brother and sister. After an emotional greeting, Bonnie and Jacob grabbed her suitcase and led her to their waiting car.

Ramona was aware of the differences in their outward appearances because her brother and sister were both dressed in the latest style of clothing that she had only seen in the pattern books at the dry goods store in Springfield. Bonnie was wearing a loose-fitting dress with a drop waist worn by a new breed of woman called the flapper. Her small brimmed hat sported a colorful peacock feather that perched jauntily in the front over spit curls that peeked out around her smiling face. Several long strands of beads swished together as she nearly skipped with happiness at having her little sister with her again. Jacob looked dapper in his suit, tie, and shiny, black leather shoes. He wore a hat with a large brim that dipped down over his sparkling brown eyes, and the chain of his pocket watch dangled from a slit in his pinstriped vest.

Ramona wasn't so sure that this was the same brother and sister who had left Springfield five years before and began to doubt the wisdom of her decision to stay the entire summer. However, it didn't take long to discover that the Polk family ties were still strong and intact and that the summer would be an adventure after all. The polished leather seats and chrome headlights of their automobile seemed to herald their entry onto the streets of an amazingly bustling town. Ramona's eyes were swimming with tears of joy as she gleefully observed the myriad of colors and patterns on the clothing featured in the windows of the famous Emery, Byrd, and Thayer Department Store.

Suddenly, as if Ramona awakened from a dream, she felt awkward about the prospect of eating at a restaurant with her brother and sister. Her dress had been made from flour sacks that her mother had skillfully sewed together into a neat-looking jumper, but her starched, white blouse was wrinkled from the oppressive heat in the passenger car. Noticing that her sister had become quiet, Bonnie asked if Ramona was feeling well enough to eat at their favorite Italian restaurant, which was within walking distance of their three-story apartment building. Ramona wasn't accustomed to telling a lie, so she blurted out that she wasn't dressed to go out to eat and take the chance of meeting any of their friends. Bonnie only laughed reassuringly and suggested that they tour the apartment and Ramona could choose one of her dresses to wear out that evening. Bonnie was several inches shorter than Ramona, but the drop waist and longer hemlines of her fashionable dresses could accommodate the difference in their heights.

As they parked in front of the stone apartment buildings, Ramona delightfully observed the colorful plants spilling over the edges of the stone flower boxes on each level of the apartments. A magnificent bronze statue of a horse and angelic rider was positioned in the center of a grassy area separating the one-way streets in the front of their apartment window. Water was gushing out of the mouth of the horse, and the rider held a spear in his right hand, seemingly ready to spear an unseen foe. It appeared to have been placed especially for the Polks to enjoy as they looked out onto the busy thoroughfare.

The apartment was spacious, and her brother and sister had bought tasteful furniture to decorate each room with pleasant but homey décor. Shiny hardwood floors framed the beautiful oriental rugs that graced each room, and brass lamps with stained glass shades lit the paneling with a soft, rose-colored hue. The only piece of furniture that was reminiscent of their childhood held a place of status in the kitchen. Martha Ellen had given Bonnie the one piece of furniture she longed for because it reminded her of the many pies she had cooked for the family throughout her teenage years. There in the corner by the china cabinet stood the beautifully polished pecan pie safe filled with delicious pies. The grate covering each level of the safe provided a peephole into which a hungry pie lover could look and select the pie of his/her choice. A twinge of homesickness momentarily walked across Ramona's feelings of joy when she saw the pie safe, but that didn't last long because her sister had raided her clothes closet and was holding up several beautiful dresses for Ramona to try on in her very own bedroom.

It was an incredible luxury to be able to shut the door and try on her new clothes without one of her younger sisters staring at her. It didn't take her long to yank off her cotton jumper and rumpled shirt before pulling a soft, dark green dress over her head and admiring herself in the floor-length mirror that hung on the back of the door. Bonnie handed her several strands of pearl-like beads that reached nearly to her knees and a pair of nylons on which a black, embroidered snake curved gracefully up the left stocking. Her sister's shoes were a little tight, but Ramona was ready to ignore some discomfort in order to look like the mannequins she had seen in the store windows earlier that day.

Ramona awkwardly stepped out into the living room for her brother and sister to see her transformation. "Wow," was all her brother could say because the beautiful young lady who appeared before him didn't look like at all like the kid sister who had met them at the train station just a few hours before. An apartment this size was a financial stretch for Jacob and Bonnie, but it was worth the cost to see the happiness in their little sister's face. Life on the farm had been hard on Ramona, and maybe a few months in the city would help her make the adjustment back into the classroom that fall and be more able to withstand the caustic remarks that were sure to be thrown her way by their father. Jacob and Bonnie both held a special place in their hearts for their little sister because she seemed to be the most sensitive of the Polk children and the one who was the most vulnerable.

Ramona would be staying in the back apartment, which had a fire escape leading to the ground level right outside the apartment's back door and a narrow walkway on which Bonnie and Jacob had slept during the intense heat of the summer. It faced the skyline of the city, and Ramona could wake up each morning to the sun peeking over the tops of buildings of the city she grew to love.

After Bonnie showed her little sister how to apply lipstick and rouge for the first time, the happy threesome locked arms and met the challenge of the city with the Polk pioneer spirit. The night was chilly after the rainfall that afternoon, and Ramona shivered from the cool air hitting her exposed arms. She was not allowed to wear the new sleeveless fashions when she was on the farm, so it was a completely new experience to have exposed arms in public. She felt vulnerable and wickedly modern at the same time.

As she entered the restaurant with her brother and sister, all eyes seemed to be riveted on her. At once, Ramona felt embarrassed and ashamed of the attention she was receiving from every male who observed her entrance into the restaurant. Her large breasts, small waist, and rounded hips were accentuated by the clinging material and strategically placed tucks that were common to this new flapper sensation. It took all of Ramona's courage to walk among the ogling men and be seated along with her sister and brother at a table in the corner.

Red and white checked tablecloths covered each table, with a lit candle flickering in the middle of each one. Ramona had never eaten a meal in a restaurant and was unsure of the manner in which she was to act. She had also never ordered off of a menu and did not recognize the names of the various Italian dishes that were listed on a backdrop of an Italian country scene. Bonnie suggested that she order the spaghetti and meatball dish that came with a side order of garlic bread and a generous portion of the house salad. She did not realize how hungry she was because of the excitement of the day and was delighted to delve into the delicious-looking meal.

She and Bonnie drank deeply from their tall wine glasses filled with a refreshingly delicious drink called Coca-Cola. Jacob pulled a flask from the inside of his coat pocket and poured the honey-colored liquid into his soda.

Halfway during the meal, a friend of Ramona's brother and sister came over to their table with a rather gaunt-looking young woman hanging possessively on his arm. Her platinum-colored finger waves poked out from under a modern-looking, black felt hat, and her bright red lips seemed to form the perfect letter O. A black mole graced the left side of her cheek near a rather deep dimple, and her ample breasts threatened to fall out of her fashionably low neckline at any minute. Ramona's sister introduced their friend as Victor Baxter, an acquaintance they had met through his mother, Gus, when they lived at her boardinghouse for a short time before moving into their own apartment. He had tried to date Bonnie, but she was not interested in going out with my future father.

Victor's eyes could not leave Ramona's face as her brother and sister tried to carry on a conversation with him. It must have been apparent that he was smitten with their younger sister because they made a point to stress the fact that Ramona was only fourteen years old and that she was visiting for the summer months before returning back to Springfield and school in the fall. Victor was in his mid-twenties and had already lived a lifetime in a hedonistic lifestyle, but he was constantly in search of the innocence of youth when choosing his next date. His raw desire for Ramona's youthful beauty must have been apparent as he intently gazed at her because his date pulled at his arm and insisted that they return to their table, where their meal was beginning to get cold.

Ramona felt an ominous cloud of fear settling over her spirit and could not understand why she no longer felt the youthful enthusiasm she had experienced at the beginning of the evening. Several times during the evening, she noticed the young man with the slicked-back, dark hair and square jaw staring at her across the room. She suddenly lost her appetite and was grateful when her brother and sister suggested that they return to the apartment and spend the rest of the night visiting and listening to the news on their newly purchased Motorola radio. This relief was short-lived, however, because Victor jumped up from his table and caught them as they were leaving the restaurant.

He asked if he could come by the apartment after he dropped his date off, and Jacob gladly told him that he was welcome to come by and visit. Bonnie felt her sister's reluctance at having him visit with them on her first night in Kansas City, so she politely spoke up and told Victor that another night would be preferable because her sister was tired and would probably want to go to sleep early. He must have noticed Ramona's relief because he rather graciously agreed to come by the next day and drive them around Kansas City in his brand-new Packard Sedan. Ramona tried to protest this intrusion into her visit, but her sister and brother appeared to be pleased with the idea of having a personal tour guide who was willing to provide the transportation to entertain their little sister. Even though they had detected a more-than-casual interest in Ramona, it never occurred to them that their friend had other than innocent thoughts about their little sister. Only Ramona, in her subconscious mind, sensed that this was a man whom she had to keep a healthy distance from and that she could never safely be with him by herself.

Later, when she and her sister were sitting on her bed talking, Ramona shared her misgivings about their friend, and Bonnie pointed out that their nine-year age difference was enough to keep Victor from being interested in her other than wanting to be nice to their kid sister as a friendly gesture. Ramona wasn't so sure her sister was correct in assuming that he was quite harmless but soon forgot her misgivings about the next day as she lay down and fell asleep almost immediately.

The morning sun cast a brilliant glow on her dark, wood-paneled walls as the mournful cry of a dove cast a pall over Ramona's usually upbeat spirit. It wasn't until she shook off her usual morning grogginess that she realized why she might be having second thoughts about the plans for that day. She didn't feel comfortable around Victor, and she would tell her brother and sister that she would rather be with just them after they returned to the apartment that evening.

She heard voices from the kitchen as she jumped out of bed and ran a brush through her unruly blond curls. Her joy was cut short, however, when she heard two men's voices talking with her sister and realized that Victor had arrived early to take them on their trip around the city. The grandfather clock sitting at the end of the hall chimed nine times, and Ramona was shocked when she realized that she had slept so late.

She slipped on another one of the dresses that Bonnie had hung in her closet the night before and twirled around several times in front of the mirror to make sure the image in the mirror was truly her and not a dream that she would wake up from. It had a sailor collar that fit over a navy blue and white striped bodice that was separated from the solid navy skirt by a red patent leather belt. A military-looking navy cap completed the fashionable ensemble, and she slipped her feet into a pair of the most beautiful, opened-toed, white, wedge heels that she had ever seen. Her sister had apparently been shopping for her for quite some time and had surprised her with a clothes closet full of the latest styles.

After applying a light coating of makeup and some mauve lipstick, Ramona walked into the kitchen, expecting to see her brother, sister, and Victor drinking cups of coffee and ready to walk out of the door and into the day's adventure. Instead, Bonnie had received a phone call from her boyfriend and had left the apartment without any explanation a few minutes earlier, and only her brother and Victor were left to take her out on the town. Jacob asked Victor if he minded picking up his girlfriend and they would all four check out the Kansas City area.

Ramona's heart fell when she realized she would have to sit in the front with Victor while her brother sat in the back with Marie, his girlfriend. This was turning into her worst nightmare, and nothing she could say or do would save her from this situation. She wished she could take the next train back to Springfield that afternoon but was afraid of hurting her sister's feelings after she had spent so much time and money in preparation for her visit.

Jacob asked her if she would like her favorite breakfast of bacon and eggs, but her stomach began to churn. She wondered if she would be able to go with them after all. Apparently, Victor wasn't going to take no for an answer because he glowered at Ramona as she clutched at her stomach. He growled, "Surely you aren't going to say that you don't want to go after I changed my plans for the day to accommodate you and your family!" Immediately, she felt as though she was back at the farm in Springfield enduring her father's scathing remarks. Tears filled her eyes as she dismissed herself to go to the bathroom.

As she shut the bathroom door, a wave of nausea washed over her, and she threw up in the sink. Fear and confusion over the situation filled her emotions as she considered the options she might have to face if she offended her brother's friend any more than what she had done. After a few minutes of overpowering despair over her lack of choices, she resolutely decided to face the day with determination and youthful resiliency.

A soft knock at the door brought her back to her senses. Jacob had begun to worry about her when she didn't immediately return to the living room. He realized that Victor had overstepped his boundaries when his request for her to go with them had turned into a demand. She was still a young girl who had been entrusted to his and his sister's care, and he had failed to make her feel safe.

He couldn't shake the ominous feeling that this wasn't a good situation and had decided to tell his little sister that she wasn't obligated to go with them unless Bonnie could go too. He was prepared to ask Victor to postpone their outing until Ramona felt better and was shocked when his sister opened the door and announced that she was ready to go. He could see she had been crying and felt horribly guilty about being a part of any unhappiness that she was feeling. He had only wanted to make her feel comfortable and happy about her visit with them. His dark brown eyes were filled with hurt as she brushed him aside and resolutely entered the room in which Victor was nervously pacing the floor.

She wondered why he seemed to be so angry about the time they were "wasting" when he had supposedly set aside the whole day to entertain her and her brother and sister. As his eyes traveled up and down her youthful curves, he took on the appearance of a hungry wolf. Ramona felt uncomfortable and ashamed at the obvious lustful thoughts of this stranger and vowed that this would be the one and only time she would be coerced into being a part of a situation in which he was present.

Her brother warily entered the room behind her and observed his friend's body language. This was a disgusting turn of events, and he was determined to find time to talk with Victor about the situation before the day was over. Victor asked if Ramona was ready to go, and without uttering a word, she stood up a little taller as she stalked toward the door with her two escorts marching behind her.

Much to Ramona's relief, Jacob opened the back door of the sedan for her to sit and climbed up into the passenger's seat. Victor stared angrily at Jacob until he realized he was the reason for what he considered his friend's display of overprotectiveness. In his world, any woman was fair game, and it wasn't up to her family to protect her against the consequences of "normal instincts." It did not occur to him that there were certain situations in which the female prey was considered out-of-bounds no matter what her age might be.

Victor pushed his sleeves up and jumped out of the car when he realized Jacob wasn't going to crank the engine. Always before, it was his friend's choice to start the engine, and he figured that today wasn't going to be any different. In his confusion, his foot slipped off the car runner, and he let out a string of expletives that solidified Ramona's opinion of this stranger who already seemed to lay claim to her. She remembered the childhood chant, "Finder's keepers; loser's weepers," and wondered why this saying would run through her mind at this time. She might have taken it as a warning from God if she had been listening a little more closely to the preacher in her mother's church.

Ramona was saved at an early age predominately because she was afraid of the consequences of not being counted as "one of the flock," and her walk with the Lord had protected her from many situations that might have possibly threatened to harden her heart. It was a very strong possibility that this was an omen from above because an overwhelming fear gripped her senses and tightened her chest until it became hard to breathe. It was only when her brother turned around and smiled reassuringly that she began to regain her composure and accept the fact that she might have fun with her brother in spite of the presence of this person who just seemed to appear from out of nowhere to impact her day.

The car began to purr, and Victor effortlessly jumped back behind the wheel, all the while pushing the starched sleeves back down onto his arms. He fumbled unsuccessfully at the buttons on the sleeves, so he turned to Ramona and asked her if she would mind buttoning his shirt before they started on their way into the city. She met his eyes with obvious defiance but reluctantly obeyed his request because she knew that the sooner they started their journey, the sooner the day would end and she could return to the apartment and the safety of her family.

As Ramona finished buttoning the last button, she noticed the muscular hands and long fingers of Jacob's friend and marveled at the strange reactions that her body seemed to be having toward this stranger. Obviously, his hands were those of a man who had been used to hard work, and she was raised with the idea that hard work was a virtue. Maybe Victor had one saving grace, even though it paled in comparison with the other personality flaws he seemed to possess. She sat back with a sigh against the rear seat, ready to endure whatever the day held in store for them.

After what seemed like an eternity of traveling through the maze of city streets, Victor pulled up in front of a two-story house in the midst of town. There was an attractive sign in the front yard proclaiming the availability of clean rooms for those who could afford the rent. Jacob explained that these large houses had become a burden to many of the owners because they were oftentimes poorly insulated and had initially been built without the electric wiring necessary to support indoor lighting. The enormous coal furnaces that demanded a continual feast of the dirty black chunks posed an ever-threatening fear of frozen water pipes during the long winter months. If there wasn't a person in the house who was young enough to physically shovel coal into the yawning mouths of the iron monsters that resided in the basements of most of the houses in the downtown areas of Kansas City, no one could possibly inhabit these homes from October to late spring. As the times grew harder, many families who owned these turn-of-the century, Victorian-style houses turned them into boardinghouses complete with running water and electric lights until they could afford the new steam heat that didn't depend quite as much on the enormous amounts of coal required for the traditional iron furnaces.

This particular boardinghouse catered to nurses-in-training and was more pleasant in its appearance than those houses surrounding it. Ramona was surprised to see how beautifully landscaped the front yard was, with two rather large flower beds on either side of the walkway leading up to the front steps of the house. Iris, hollyhocks, roses, and several other colorful flowers were already blooming in the carefully manicured beds. It was especially early for the hollyhocks to be blooming, but Ramona figured that the warmth of the sun against the white, cement foundation of the house created a heat panel that tricked the flowers into thinking it was much later in the summer. Someone had trimmed the yard earlier that morning because there were bits of grass lying on the sidewalk, and the smell of freshly cut lawn still hung in the air.

Ramona was enjoying the beauty of the moment so completely that she hadn't noticed her brother's girlfriend until she bounced out of the front door and was standing at the car window next to Jacob. She had been waiting for them to get there and ran out of the house before Jacob had time to meet her at the front door. Marie was short and rather pleasantly plump, with deep dimples and snappy brown eyes. A lightweight pale yellow sweater draped gracefully over the shoulders of her dark brown and white striped, dropped-waist dress, and her chocolate brown crochet cap hugged her short, auburn finger waves. Her face broke into an infectious smile as Jacob turned to acknowledge her presence at his door and to wrap her in his famous bear hug.

As he opened the back door to let her sit beside his little sister, Ramona detected the disappointment in Marie's demeanor and confusion in her eyes. Normally, Jacob would have sat beside her as he held her hand, but today he had met her eyes with a look that bordered on an urgency that she did not understand. Her intuition told her that her boyfriend's actions had something to do with Victor and his little sister, but she had learned long ago not to press her personal agenda when Jacob was dealing with his own emotionally charged situations. He was a quiet man who would only share his own feelings after much coercion on her part, and she did not want to question his motives in front of others.

After they had gone the length of the block, Marie resolutely sat back in the seat and began to chat with the beautiful younger sister of the man who had stolen her heart the first time she had met him at a factory picnic.

After walking down Petticoat Lane in downtown Kansas City, the young foursome wandered into the Forum Cafeteria to eat a quick lunch and shop for some incidentals at Woolworth's five- and ten-cent store afterward. Ramona's mother had not sent Ramona with much money for necessities, so she would have to be frugal in her spending habits. Victor insisted that he pay for all four meals at the cafeteria, so Jacob declared that he would buy a tank of gas at the end of the day.

Ramona had never seen such a display of food as she encountered that day in the restaurant. Her plate was piled high with so much food when she reached the cashier that she blushed a bright red as he added up her ticket. Victor glared at her apparent lack of self-discipline and sullenly ate his own meal as Ramona, her brother, and his girlfriend carried on a continuous chatter of happy conversation.

As Ramona finished the last bite of her chocolate cake, Victor jumped up and announced that it was time to check out the five- and ten-cent store and perhaps take in a movie at the new and luxurious Embassy Theater. Ramona had only heard about the new talkies and was excited about experiencing this modern form of entertainment before she realized that she might have to sit next to Victor in a darkened theater. Marie noticed the change in Ramona's demeanor, so she asked Ramona if she would rather visit the zoo than go to the movies. Ramona gratefully responded with a relieved yes! Victor resolutely understood that he was outnumbered and trudged behind the other three on their way back to his highly polished sedan.

Later, as the four walked between the animal cages at

the Kansas City Zoo, Victor fell into step with Ramona and clumsily tried to start a conversation with her about her life in Springfield. Jacob and Marie walked arm in arm in front of Ramona and Victor, which left Ramona with the choice of either ignoring Victor's small talk or to engage him into a conversation about the animals that seemed to be more interested in eating than performing for the zoo visitors. Fortunately for Ramona, both she and Victor were interested in animals, so they were able to comfortably share their mutual experiences without feeling awkward or stiff. Ramona was pleasantly surprised to find out that Victor was tremendously knowledgeable about most of the animals at the zoo, so the afternoon passed pleasantly, with very few moments of awkward silence.

After several hours had passed, Marie announced that she should be heading to the house because she was scheduled to take a test on the circulation system the next day. Victor opened his mouth to contradict Marie's request to end the day, but Jacob shot him a look that stopped any further comments about the subject. They all turned back toward the car as the afternoon sun dropped behind the trees growing on the Missouri River bluffs.

Ramona's new shoes had worn a nasty blister on the backs of both of her heels, and she painfully slipped them off as soon as she sat down in the car. Marie's medical experience made it clear to her that Ramona should soak her feet as soon as she got back to the apartment and should avoid wearing her new shoes until her feet healed completely. Victor's eyes showed disdain for Ramona's dilemma, as if she were responsible for the condition of her feet instead of being disturbed about the pain that was shooting up her legs in increasing intensity. His reaction confused everyone in the car, but no one seemed to care how he felt unless it interfered with them reaching their respective homes before much later.

Without another word, Victor swung his car out onto Swope Parkway and headed toward Marie's boardinghouse and eventual freedom to undertake the activities of the night that were much more enjoyable to him than those he had experienced earlier that day. He felt a sudden urge to take his passengers home as quickly as possible, so he drove as fast as he could through the side streets and alleys that ran behind the brick-faced buildings of the city. Several times during the journey, Victor turned the wheel of his automobile so suddenly to avoid wrecking into piled rubbish that the car jerked violently and threatened to careen off the road and into the curb. Jacob reminded him that he had promised to buy his gas, but Victor assured him that there would be another chance in the near future to fill his tank.

The passengers were relieved when Victor deposited each one of them at their homes and quickly sped away to enjoy the rest of his evening. Ramona carried her shoes and held on to Jacob's arm as she limped up the steps and into the security of the apartment. Bonnie had arrived home several hours before and met her sister and brother at the door with a smile on her lips and an engagement ring on her finger. Her boyfriend, Samuel, had proposed earlier that day during a walk in the park, and Bonnie could hardly wait for them to return home so she could share her exciting news.

Ramona had not met her sister's fiancé in person but felt as though she already knew him from the letters Bonnie faithfully wrote to her. He had extended an invitation to all three of them to attend dinner at his mother's house the next evening, but because he was scheduled to work that afternoon, he requested that Jacob bring both sisters to his home so they could all get acquainted with both him and his mother.

Jacob appeared more quiet than usual the rest of the evening, until Bonnie questioned him about what had happened that afternoon. He told her about how Victor had acted toward Ramona and how he let his little sister sit in the backseat while they drove into town. He did not feel like it was a good idea to let Victor feel like he could drop by the apartment any time he felt inclined to do so because their little sister felt uncomfortable around him. He had not been a frequent visitor in the past, and Jacob wanted to keep it that way in spite of Bonnie's argument that he was the son of a woman who was willing to rent them a room when others wouldn't after they first moved to Kansas City.

Ramona felt uncomfortable being the cause of any dissension between her older brother and sister, so she decided to excuse herself and turn in for the night. As she was shutting her bedroom door, she heard Jacob ask his sister how she expected him to keep up the apartment rent for the rest of the summer if she planned to marry Sam before Ramona was to return to Springfield in the fall. Bonnie hadn't thought of an answer to this dilemma, but she assured Jacob that she would come up with an answer after she discussed it with Samuel the next day. Ramona fell asleep rather quickly after she soaked her aching feet in soda water and applied iodine to the open sores that were left after the blisters burst on the backs of her heels. She slept restlessly as confusing dreams robbed her of a much-needed night of relaxed rest.

Morning came much too early as she awoke to the rumbling of an approaching early summer storm. The high winds were scraping the gnarled limbs of a nearby tree against the screen covering her bedroom window, and the first raindrops landed on the dust that lightly covered the windowsill near her bed. She made a mental note to dust her room when she arose, but it was such a comfortably snug feeling to pull her covers up to her chin and watch the increasing strength of the storm moving toward her that she lost track of time and forgot that she was supposed to accompany Bonnie and Jacob to the early church service.

The apartment seemed unusually quiet when she finally decided to get out of bed and join her family for a bowl of cereal and a hot cup of coffee. It was dark in the kitchen because the cloud cover had blocked out the sunlight, and none of the lights in the living room or the kitchen were turned on. Ramona glanced at the clock on the kitchen wall and was disappointed that she had missed going to church with her brother and sister.

Ramona decided she would ease into the day with the help of a relaxing tub of hot water and bath salts when a loud knock at the front door interrupted the tranquility of her morning. Feeling totally alone and helpless, Ramona slipped on her robe and tiptoed to the front door. Her breath caught in her throat as she stood completely still with her ear against the door. She jumped back and fell against the umbrella stand that stood by the door as the knocking became more intense. It was no use to pretend that the apartment was uninhabited, so Ramona reluctantly opened the door a tiny crack to see who was responsible for the intense pounding.

Anger and disappointment flooded her senses when she recognized the person responsible for ruining her morning plans. There stood Victor with his hand still balled up into a fist ready to attack the door with another barrage of pounding. His face was contorted into an angry mask of determination as his left eye began to wink with an uncontrollable tic. The man standing before Ramona was so completely out of control that it would have been funny if the situation weren't so personal.

"What do you want?" was all Ramona could think to say before her unwanted visitor angrily pushed open the door to let himself in. Before Victor took another step into the apartment, Ramona told him to leave and demanded that he call next time to make sure her brother was there before he decided to visit. Victor had not been used to women shutting a door in his face once they realized he was a determined sort of chap, so he was taken completely off guard by this mere slip of a country girl. Suddenly, Victor awkwardly turned and ran down the steps to his automobile without so much as a glance back at Ramona.

The second wave of wind and rain began to beat on the pavement and darken the sky as the back lights on

Victor's car disappeared in the distance, leaving Ramona so weak that she slid down the door and sat on the floor until she could regain her composure and quiet her breathing enough to lock the front door and slip into her warm bathwater. She could hardly wait to tell her brother and sister what had happened because she felt that they would surely agree to discourage Victor's visits, and then perhaps she would not have to be confronted with this type of situation again.

After the church service, Bonnie and Jacob arrived back at the apartment, where the delicious smell of lunch hung in the air and a merry tune played on the Victrola. Bonnie kicked off her shoes and followed the smell that had met them at the front door. Jacob went to his bedroom to call Marie to see how well she had done on her medical exam and to hang up his suit coat before joining the girls for lunch.

As Bonnie entered the kitchen, Ramona met her with a homemade menu in her hand and a wooden spoon in the other. After a rather gallant bow, Ramona gestured toward a table filled with a variety of delicious-looking food that had been prepared and arranged on a most delightfully decorated table. Ramona had sliced the roast beef into delectably thin pieces and had made a tantalizing French gravy to pour over the perfectly mashed potatoes dripping with farm fresh butter. A crisp green salad filled the silver serving bowl with a myriad of colors, and one of Bonnie's pies had been cut into pieces and set on individual china serving plates and placed at the tip of each shiny fork. An assortment of flowers peeked out of one of the family antique vases in the middle of the table as a thin white candle burned warmly in the crystal candleholder next to the vase. Jacob came wandering in after he assured his girlfriend that he would be calling her back after lunch and was also delighted at Ramona's contribution to their Sunday afternoon.

After the three had eaten lunch and were relaxing in the living room, Ramona began to tell them what happened after they had left for church that morning. Anger clouded her brother's eyes as Ramona told him about how Victor tried to push his way into the apartment after she did not ask him to come in and that she had to tell him to leave and not come back unless someone in the family was present. Bonnie assured Ramona that she had done the right thing, but she thought Victor was harmless and that he was welcome to visit when either she or her brother were in the apartment. Jacob opened his mouth to protest, but Bonnie shot him a look that said, "Be quiet." He stoically sat in his chair watching the fear in his little sister's eyes as she told how violently Victor had smashed the door with his fist.

Bonnie abruptly ended the conversation with a reminder that they had but a few short hours before they would leave to meet Samuel's mother, and she wanted them all to be in a good mood. She jumped up and offered to help Ramona with the lunch dishes, but her little sister insisted that Bonnie take a nap while she finished cleaning up the kitchen. Bonnie excused herself and closed the door to her bedroom so she could relax and dream of the happy life that lay ahead of her. Jacob followed Ramona into the kitchen to lend a hand and talk more about the situation that had obviously compromised his sister's safety and to inform her that he was ready to tell Victor not to come around the apartment anymore.

Bonnie did not know much about her friend, but because he seemed generous and friendly when he visited his mother at the boardinghouse, she was open to letting him drop by the apartment occasionally and going with him to the movies when she wasn't going out with Sam. Sam knew Bonnie was enthusiastic about life and didn't like to sit home every evening while he worked at his route, so he had told her it was all right with him if Victor went along with her as long as she paid her own way. Jacob and Marie accompanied them on most of their outings anyway, so the situation seemed to be a perfect solution to keep his girlfriend from getting bored on the nights she would have been sitting home alone by herself.

Jacob didn't feel comfortable around Victor, however, because his explosive personality had gotten them into several volatile situations. He was a quiet man who didn't have to be entertained, so it was primarily because of Bonnie that he and Marie went out with Victor and his sister in the first place. It wouldn't bother him at all not to ever see Victor again, and he would talk to Bonnie in the next few days about his concerns over his sister's safety and ask her to let him tell Victor not to come to the apartment again.

As the two sisters and their brother pulled up in front of a beautifully ornate Victorian-style house complete with an antique gas lamp casting a rosy glow over meticulously kept flower gardens and a white gazebo, Sam opened the front door and bounded down a rather long flight of stone steps. He shook hands warmly with Jacob and turned to be introduced to their little sister. His sparkling blue eyes danced with happiness as he led them into his childhood home and into the presence of one of the most grim-faced women Ramona had ever met. Her tightly set lips and cold gray eyes presented the exact opposite persona than that of her gregarious son. In fact, her apparent disappointment in her son's choice of a future wife seemed to border on disdain for the three Polk siblings, who were awkwardly trying to make small talk. It was obvious that she would have preferred a wife of social standing for her son and that he had purposefully gone against her wishes.

Samuel ignored his mother's less-than-cordial attitude and went about making things as pleasant as he could for his company. He grabbed Bonnie's hand as he led the tour through each elegantly furnished room while occasionally pausing to tell an especially poignant story about certain ancestors who peered down at them from their oil canvases. His mother was never far behind, as though she were afraid that one of Sam's friends might steal a valuable collectible.

Almost immediately after the Polks arrived, Sam's mother, Mrs. Vanderson, cleared her throat and announced that dinner would be served in the dining room after the guests washed their hands. The chocolate-skinned maid fluttered around the lavishly set table while Sam's mother indicated the seating arrangement. Sam was to be seated next to her while Bonnie was to be seated on the other side of Ramona. This wasn't Samuel's choice, but he agreed to placate his mother so she wouldn't wreak havoc with the rest of the evening.

Bonnie's eyes filled with tears as she sat down the table from her fiancé, and the realization began to dawn on her that Sam's loyalty to his mother meant more to him than his relationship with her. Whether it was his love of money or his craving for the social status his mother had acquired throughout the years, eventually, his mother won out, and their future marriage lasted less than two years. This was the first indication to Bonnie that she would never be first in her future husband's life, but Sam vehemently promised that his love for Bonnie outweighed his loyalty to his mother and that Mrs. Vanderson would grow to love his future wife as much as he did.

Nonetheless, a pall had fallen over the rest of the evening, and almost immediately after dinner had been consumed without much conversation, Jacob announced that he had to get to sleep early so he could wake up refreshed the next day, ready to tackle his job at the factory. No one objected except Sam, but he was quickly shushed by Mrs. Vanderson, who smiled faintly at the prospect of spending the rest of the evening alone with her only son.

Stiff good-byes were exchanged, and the three Polk siblings nearly bounded down the front steps in their effort to escape the discomfort of the evening. Sam followed Bonnie down the stairs and grabbed her before she stepped into the front seat beside Jacob. He groaned with sorrow as he realized how hurt his fiancée had been over his mother's actions and promised her that it would never happen again. Bonnie wasn't convinced, but as Sam's lips touched hers in a goodnight kiss, she forgot the pain of the evening and was looking forward to planning their summer wedding.

She and Ramona could plan the wedding together, and the summer would be filled with the excitement of choosing the furnishings and décor for her new home as well as the flowers that would decorate her mid-summer wedding.

Victor did not visit their apartment again until several days before the wedding. He brought a wedding present for Bonnie and a huge arrangement of flowers for their kitchen table. Jacob had left that morning for a date with Marie, and Ramona was asked to answer the door while her sister discussed the service with the church's pastor. Ramona's breath caught in her throat when she realized who was standing in front of her, but Victor made it quite clear by his actions that she wasn't the one for whom this visit was intended. His demeanor was quite different from that of the last visit, and he didn't seem to be interested in her presence at all. In fact, it was as though she were nothing more than one of the light fixtures in the room. Ramona was so relieved that she relaxed and told Victor to have a seat until her sister was through talking on the phone to the pastor.

Bonnie cut her conversation to the pastor a little shorter than expected, but she felt that her brother wouldn't want Ramona left by herself with Victor for any length of time. She didn't want to make Jacob mad before the wedding. Arrangements had been made to accommodate her family at a local hotel, and they would be arriving the next morning. She had planned to ask several of their friends if they would mind driving her family around town and to the church for the wedding. Victor would be a perfect driver because he knew the downtown area so well, and he always seemed to want to please Bonnie. It had occurred to Ramona on several occasions to ask Bonnie if she thought that he secretly carried a torch for her, but the time never seemed right to breach the subject, and now it was too late.

Saturday morning came early, and Bonnie nervously dressed in a light pink silk suit with the brim of an elegant straw hat gracefully dipping down over her right eye. A large, silk pink rose peeked out from under a dark green velvet band that encircled the crown of the hat, and a double strand of pearls fell gracefully inside the curved neckline of her blouse. Ramona had gotten dressed before her sister because she wanted to help Bonnie prepare for her important day.

Their mother and father, sisters, and younger brother had arrived by car the night before, and they had stayed up late visiting. Ramona wanted to caution her sister about the dark circles brushing faintly against her lower eyelids, but she didn't want to alarm Bonnie about anything that would take away from the joy she was feeling on her special day. Consequently, she helped Bonnie with her makeup before they walked out the front door and took special care to pat an extra puff of face powder under her sister's eyes so that her outward appearance would radiate the inner enthusiasm that she felt for her impending marriage.

Victor was punctual as usual and had already picked up Bonnie's family from the hotel and let them off at the church. Cliff and Jeremy, the other two Polk brothers, had arrived together with their wives and were sitting in the second row of the sanctuary when Victor arrived with the rest of the family.

The church was decorated tastefully with beautiful white and pink roses cascading down two brass candelabras, and another immense bouquet of baby's breath and pink tea roses had been placed in the middle of the baptismal that opened up high above the pulpit. It almost seemed a shame that such a beautifully decorated sanctuary would be viewed by so few guests because Bonnie and Jacob had not lived in Kansas City long enough to have made many friends, and Mrs. Vanderson had refused to invite any of her socially prominent acquaintances. They had prepared for relatively few guests to attend the wedding reception that had been arranged for by Sam's mother at the opulent Muelbach Hotel in downtown Kansas City, and it was just as well because Jeff and Ellen left with the younger children to return to Springfield as soon as the ceremony was over.

Gus Holbert and her two daughters, Maxine and Stella, were escorted down the aisle to be seated on Bonnie's side of the church. Their brazen stares at the males in the congregation reminded Ramona of the way Victor had looked at her, and a cold shudder ran between her shoulder blades and down the entire length of her spine before she was jolted out of her thoughts by a commotion that was taking place outside of the church doors. She had not been seated with her family yet because she was the maid of honor and would not sit with them until she finished her part in the ceremony.

As she turned around to look at where the noise was coming from, she saw Sam rushing toward the Lincoln Touring car that had arrived carrying his mother and her maid. It appeared that Mrs. Vanderson had twisted her ankle while exiting her automobile and was intent on delaying the wedding until she had her doctor evaluate the damage. It seemed strange to Ramona that when Sam's mother thought no one was looking, she put weight on her sprained ankle without even so much as a wince. Ramona shook off those thoughts because it was inconceivable to her that Mrs. Vanderson would be so self-centered on her son's wedding day that she was willing to change the entire course of events to satisfy her own needs.

Sam asked the preacher if he could wait a few minutes to start the ceremony until he figured out what should be done about his mother's injury. No one noticed that Victor's mother, Gus, had gotten up out of her seat and had parted the crowd that had formed around Mrs. Vanderson. She was used to taking control because she had owned and run her own boardinghouse ever since her husband had died and was ready to take over the situation on that day. Also, because my grandmother Gus was no stranger to these kinds of misinterpretations of the truth, she sensed that Mrs. Vanderson was being less than candid about what had happened outside the church doors. She had her own plans to have her lawn cut that afternoon and was impatient about sitting through any church service, let alone one that might last much longer than expected. She also sensed that if this ceremony didn't progress as planned, her friend Bonnie might call the whole thing off, and she would have gotten dressed up for nothing.

Stella had bought her and Maxine very expensive suits from Rothschild's Department Store the week before, and Gus had reluctantly agreed to dress up in the fancy attire in order to be presentable. Her plans were to immediately replace the suit with one of her many flowing housedresses and take her usual seat on the front porch swing of her two-story house. Her routine included engaging her neighbors in various conversations as they walked down her front sidewalk, and only the most pressing situations would keep her from her vigil.

This unforeseeable event wasn't going to change her plans, and she walked right up to the suffering mother of the groom. She whispered into her ear that if she didn't straighten up she would blow the whistle on her, and Sam would never forgive her for ruining his wedding. Mrs. Vanderson opened her mouth to object to Grandmother Gus's threatening tone of voice, but Gus just winked and turned around to return to her pew. Sam's mother was so taken aback that all she could do was grab the arm of the nearest usher and hobble to her proper position across the aisle from the Polks.

There were only a handful of Sam's friends sitting behind his mother and an empty space where his father should have been sitting beside her. Sam's mother had requested that he leave his father out of the activities, and he had agreed since Mr. Vanderson was not a part of his life and had not been since he was a very small boy. Several of Bonnie's friends had filtered in, smiled at the family, and took their seat with an air of expectation. The groom and his best man assumed their places at the front of the sanctuary and gazed toward the back of the church in anticipation. Sam didn't seem to be nervous at all as he smiled at Bonnie's family while avoiding his own mother's gaze.

The wedding march began to herald the entrance of the bride and her father as Mrs. Vanderson stared straight ahead at the burning candles and shifted nervously in her seat. A beautifully sung solo gave the cue to Jeff Polk and Bonnie to start down the aisle toward Sam. Bonnie's sparkling blue eyes did not leave Sam's face, and when Jeff handed her over to her husband-to-be, he reached over, brushed aside a lock of hair, and lightly touched her cheek with a warm kiss. Jeff also gave his eldest daughter a perfunctory kiss on her other cheek as he handed her over to her husband-to-be. He appeared to be uncomfortable in his suit, yet his youthfully slim physique and dark, wavy hair gave him the appearance of someone who should be at ease in any socially charged situation.

Women were enchanted by his good looks and aloofness, but he no longer made a habit of infidelity after the widow had married another man and moved away from Springfield. He sat stiffly and seemed to concentrate on keeping distance between himself and his wife. It was fine with his wife that he maintained an emotional distance in their marriage because Ellen had become increasingly more aloof and bitter as the years went by, and the distance between them was much farther than that which separated them on the pew.

The ceremony was tastefully short, and as the organ

music swelled to fill the entire church, Bonnie and Sam turned to leave the sanctuary and drive to the hotel as Mr. and Mrs. Samuel Vanderson. Victor and some of the other young men from Sam's company had tied shoes and tin cans to the back of Sam's Model T Ford and were waiting to congratulate them as they exited the church. Bonnie had taken time to hug her mother, father, sisters, and brothers before their departure and assured them that Jacob would take care of Ramona just fine for the rest of her visit. Sam's mother smiled cordially to the Polks and asked her maid if she would mind helping her to their car because she wasn't feeling well and had decided not to grace the wedding party with her appearance at the reception.

Sam seemed disappointed that his mother wasn't going to attend the party but did not insist that she change her mind. Instead, he made sure that she was safely on her way home before he picked up his new bride and kissed her squarely on the lips under a barrage of rice and rose petals. He and Bonnie ran to their car and drove away from the church with the tin cans clanking against the pavement and shoes bouncing against the bumper of the car. A round of good-byes ushered Jeff, Ellen, and the younger children on their way back to Springfield as the older Polk siblings looked forward to a night of fun and excitement at the Muelbach Hotel.

Ramona, Jacob, and Marie talked enthusiastically about the wedding as Victor drove them and his date to the party. Ramona couldn't help noticing how handsome Victor looked in his three-piece vested suit and brimmed hat. His shoes had been shined until they reflected the light from the incoming cars, and his gray eyes seemed to glimmer with happiness for the first time since Ramona had met him. Perhaps the joy from the events of the day had spilled over into his soul, and he felt happiness for his friend Bonnie. Whatever the reason, he had been easily drawn into the conversations around him and appeared comfortably at peace with his attractive date. Her name was Ida, and her face was constantly lit up with a charming smile as she touched his hand with hers and gazed at him with adoring eyes. Ramona was relieved that she would not have to be worried about Victor's overtures and began to excitedly anticipate the events of the night.

When Victor drove into the circular drive in front of the hotel, a uniformed valet opened the car doors and offered his hand to help the ladies out onto the curb. Ramona had never been treated with such protocol, so she didn't know quite what to do when the valet opened her door. Marie whispered that she was to offer the gentleman her hand and let him gently help her out of the car. The valet was delighted at the young girl's lack of a sense of decorum, so he was especially intent on giving her his special treatment usually reserved for those in powerful positions. With a flourish and a gallant bow, he took Ramona's hand in his and placed it on his arm as he personally walked her into the hotel. He took her to the wedding reception and introduced her by name to members of the hotel management who had been extended an invitation by Sam's mother. Ramona felt like a queen, and when it was time for the valet to leave her with her family, she blushed in the face of the attention that had been drawn to her by her unplanned escort.

Ramona took turns sitting with each of her older brothers and their wives as they talked about life on the farm and how different their lives had become since they had moved away and married. Only Cliff missed farm life and was planning to move back to Nixa, Missouri, to raise a few head of cattle and grow corn. His wife was a city girl, but she was enthusiastically agreeing to be a part of her husband's dream and help him with his plans to develop a successful farming business.

Jeremy was more of an adventurer, so his plans included traveling and working wherever he could find a job to support his next move. His wife was young and enthusiastic, so she had been excited about traveling with her husband and discovering their country firsthand. They had just returned from San Francisco, where Jeremy had worked on completing the Golden Gate Bridge, and everyone around him was listening intently to his stories about the dangers he had encountered while working high above the San Francisco Bay. Fortunately, they were able to attend the wedding because they were on their way back to her family's spread outside of Omaha, Arkansas, to rest up and plan their next adventure. Sue, Jeremy's wife, had recently been plagued with increasingly painful headaches and fatigue, so they both agreed to give her time to rest and visit with her mother and father before they took off again. But tonight they were both enjoying the festivities of the evening in spite of their nagging concerns over Sue's health.

Jacob and Marie danced to the live music of a locally

prominent band as Ramona tapped the toe of her single-strap, linen pumps to the beat of the tune. She hadn't noticed that Victor had taken his date home earlier in the evening and had returned to enjoy the rest of the evening without having to be encumbered with her. In fact, he was looking forward to befriending Ramona and possibly asking her to dance. After all, she was surrounded by three of her strapping brothers, and that should give her the security she needed to feel free to dance with him. Victor did not consider the fact that she might not know how to dance or that she might possibly want to spend the evening visiting with her family before they left the next afternoon. In fact, both assumptions were true, and as Victor walked over to Ramona to ask her to dance, she could not hide her displeasure as she turned her back to him and entered into a rather lengthy conversation with Marie about her friends in Springfield.

Victor didn't accept her obvious rejection of his advances, however, and proceeded to grab her arm and gently pull her onto the dance floor amid her polite refusals. Her brothers had been caught up in the revelry of the evening, so they did not discourage Victor's forwardness toward their little sister and nodded in agreement for him to dance with her while holding her tightly against him as he enjoyed the movement of her breasts against his body. At first, Ramona's legs felt like pieces of wood, and she clumsily fell against Victor as she tried to move to the rhythm of the music. But after a few moments of my father's hand guiding her with his tight grasp on her lower back, she began to loosen up and dance gracefully to the beat.

After a few dances, Victor led her to the refreshment table and offered to pour a little gin his mother had made into her glass of Coca-Cola to quench her thirst and loosen up her youthful inhibitions. Drinking was illegal because prohibition was in full swing, so the liquor he poured into Ramona's glass when no one was looking had been poured into a flask that slipped perfectly into a hidden pocket of Victor's vest. Even though Ramona objected to his disregard for her age and Christian principles, she decided that a few sips might actually be useful for taking away some of her uneasiness about the night. After two glasses of the gin-infused beverage, Ramona began to feel her self-control wavering and agreed to let him take her home so the other couples could visit and perhaps go out on the town later without their little sister tagging along.

Bonnie and Sam had left the party several hours before, and the other guests were beginning to thin out, so it seemed an appropriate time for them to bid their adieus and leave the festivities. Jacob did not like the idea of his sister leaving with Victor, but as was his practice, he had drank entirely too much of his own illegally acquired whiskey and gave into Victor's demands to take Ramona home with a promise that he would treat her with respect. Ramona's good judgment had been drastically impaired by the alcohol, and as she stepped into Victor's sedan, she found herself being pulled close to the driver's side by his strong and unyielding grasp. Before she had time to withdraw to her side of the car, he grabbed her face with his other hand and kissed her long and deep until she could not breathe.

At first, the unexpected gesture threw her off balance, and she drew back with terror in her eyes. Victor just grinned and drew her to himself again, this time with more urgency in his grasp and desire clouding his eyes. He rarely drank alcohol, so his reactions were clearly designed to break down Ramona's will without the clumsiness that accompanied an alcoholic funk.

As his hand began to unbutton the front of her dress, Jacob, Jeremy, and Cliff Polk appeared at the back door of the car. They had missed their chance to hail a cab, so they decided to ask Victor if he could take all three couples downtown before he let Ramona off at the apartment. Jacob's concern for his sister's safety made him question the good judgment of leaving her to fend for herself against someone as acquainted with the seedy side of life as Victor was. Nonetheless, he gave into his brothers' pleadings to accompany them for an evening out on the town and pushed his nagging feelings of doubt on the backburner to be reckoned with the next day.

Five of the squealing, shoving passengers crammed into the backseat while Jacob sat in front with Ramona and Victor. He detected a feeling of anger from Victor, as if they were intruding into a situation that was taboo for the rest of the Polk clan. The feelings of hostility emanating from Victor were so strong, in fact, that Jacob had no choice but to follow his instincts and ask that Victor take him and the rest of his family to the apartment, where they could borrow his car and continue with their revelry. Victor knew when he was outmatched, so he reluctantly agreed to drive them home without a word of hesitation.

Ramona was both relieved and confused at the feelings

of desire that had been awakened by Victor's kisses and urgent caresses. She was yet a child in her knowledge of the things of the world, and these awakening desires had caught her off guard and placed a stabbing shame in her soul. Eventually, guilt would seal her commitment to a lifetime in a loveless and emotionally painful marriage, as Victor successfully set the stage that night to pursue his fantasies at another time in the future.

The gaiety of the evening lost much of its vigor as the three front-seat passengers sat stiffly staring straight ahead. Jacob pulled Ramona close to his side, and she did not resist because this further increased the distance between her leg and Victor's thigh. The jostling of the car and the hum of the motor played into Ramona's alcohol-induced fatigue, causing her to fall asleep on her brother's shoulder nearly as soon as they pulled away from the front of the hotel. It was at this point that Jacob realized Victor had more than likely given Ramona some of Gus's homemade gin at the reception and that it was probably a timely decision to leave the party when they did.

Victor pulled up in front of the apartment and volunteered to carry Ramona up the stairs and into her bedroom, but Jacob's grim demeanor and his icy retort encouraged Victor's hasty retreat. The other members of the party shot each other questioning looks as they followed their brother and obviously drunk sister through the front door. He did not share his concerns with his brothers because he felt a stab of guilt at not protecting his young sister from an obviously demoralizing situation. It struck him that because Bonnie no longer lived in the apartment, he had more control over the situation, and he would be able to ban Victor from the apartment from that day on.

Just as Jacob was feeling relieved over his decision, Victor was feeling his loss in the most hurtful of ways and became resolved to the fact that he might not ever see Ramona again. He was so angry at his lack of good judgment and patience that he did something entirely out of character for him—he stopped his car in front of a hotel well known for its secret brothel and spent the last of his paycheck on activities that would help him detach from the loss that he felt in his heart. It would be embarrassing for his family to know that he had paid for what he usually got free, but somehow he felt like cutting to the chase without having to play the usual courting games. After several hours, he fell despondently into the front seat of his car and drove to his uncle's house with a heavy heart and an overpowering feeling of depression. He had never felt these sensations about a woman, and this left him completely confused about where his life was leading him. He fell asleep dreaming that Ramona's face was floating above his bed, and a restlessness in his heart left him angry and empty.

The evening no longer held the excitement that had penetrated the air earlier that evening, so therefore, no one felt like continuing the festivities. Instead, the family decided to stay at Jacob's apartment to visit and compare memories of their childhood. Ramona excused herself and retired to her bedroom as soon as she entered the front door so her brothers couldn't see how embarrassed she was over the events of the evening. She inwardly suspected that

Jacob would discuss the situation with their other brothers and agree to send her back to Springfield before the summer was over. Her disappointment over that possibility sent her to her knees as she prayed for God's forgiveness and a second chance to prove herself to her brother.

The longer she was away from the farm and her father's stern approach to fatherhood, the more convinced she was that she no longer could abide living in those conditions. She would beg her brother to stay and let her find a job to help pay for the apartment in return for her promise to study her school subjects and find an academy in Kansas City where she might be able to attend night classes and earn her high school degree. After she said her prayers and pulled the sheet up to her chin, Ramona fell into a deep and troubled sleep that periodically was punctuated with thoughts about her activities in the front seat with Victor. He had awakened feelings in her that she did not know existed, and a part of her yearned to experience those feelings again, but not with him.

Jacob knocked on her door the next morning and asked her to get ready for church because they were going to meet the other brothers and their wives for the service and lunch afterward. They would be parting ways after they ate, and he felt that Ramona should visit with them before they left. She reluctantly sat on the edge of the bed as her head pounded from the aftereffects of Gus's bathtub gin. She knew she had no choice but to get dressed and be ready to leave with Jacob before the hour was up, so she asked him if he could bring her a cup of coffee and an aspirin to calm her aching head.

He was an early riser, so when he appeared at her door with her requests in hand, he was fully dressed, shaved, and ready to walk out the door. There was no condemnation in his eyes as he smiled at his little sister—only sadness that somehow he had let her down. Ramona opened her mouth to let him know that what happened wasn't his fault but felt that this was neither the time nor the place to do so. Instead, she assured him that she would be ready on time, and that was exactly what she intended to do. In between sips of the strong, black coffee, she drew her summery yellow poplin dress over her head and applied her makeup just as Bonnie had taught her to do. A short-sleeved white jacket completed the smart-looking outfit, and a pair of yellow lace gloves gave a touch of youthful innocence.

When Ramona finally entered the living room ready to leave for church, she did not even resemble the wobbly, confused child-woman who had struggled to climb the steps with her brother the night before. Instead, Jacob saw before him a young woman on the verge of adulthood who was ready for whatever the world would throw at her. After what had happened the night before, he wasn't sure he was up to the responsibility of handling a teenage girl without the help of his sister. In fact, he had toyed with the idea of telling his mother and father that Ramona would be coming home with Jeremy and his wife on their way to Arkansas that afternoon but nixed the idea after he realized how disappointed she would be. Surely he could let her stay a few more weeks, and afterward, he would move into a one-bedroom apartment in the same building and get on with his life as a bachelor without anyone but himself to be responsible for. She looked so happy and full of life as they drove to the church that he was sure his decision to let her stay was the right choice and that he would not bring up the matter again until it was time for her to return to school.

As they pulled up in front of the massive church, their family members were already standing on the steps, waiting for them to arrive. When they saw how Ramona had rebounded from the night before, they seemed relieved and delighted that she had decided to join them for the afternoon. The preacher talked about sin and its impact on people's lives as Ramona's eyes filled with tears of remorse and pain. Jeremy had noticed the sorrowful expression on her face and slipped his arm around her shoulder to assure her that there were no hard feelings from him and that he knew she was everything he ever wanted in a little sister and more. Ramona was grateful for her brothers and their compassionate nature and settled back to enjoy the rest of the service with a joyful heart and hope for the future.

Afterward, they ate lunch at the cafeteria and later watched as Jeremy and Cliff drove away with their wives and a car full of packages filled with purchases for the rest of the family. Sue had developed a migraine headache during lunch and had asked if she could lie down on the backseat with her head in Jeremy's lap as they journeyed to her parents' farm in Arkansas. They both were hopeful that the clear country air would stop her more frequent headaches while Jeremy and her father built a larger barn and cleared the land to provide more pasture for the new calves that had been born that spring.

After everyone left, Ramona and Jacob drove to Marie's to take her for a ride and to ask if she would like to accompany them to a movie that was featuring a new actor, John Barrymore. Ramona crawled into the backseat while Jacob held the door for Marie to jump into the front seat and scoot over to sit close by him as he maneuvered skillfully through the evening traffic of the city. Ramona never got tired of the excitement of the city, so she was content to watch the crowds of people as they swarmed into the stores and flowed back out onto the sidewalks with bulging bags of goods purchased from their favorite boutique.

The city life suited her personality so perfectly that she was sure of her decision not to return to the farm. When the time was right, she would ask her brother if she could stay and help him pay the rent by getting a job at the Forum Cafeteria. She had noticed the "Help Wanted" sign in the window when the family went out to eat after church and secretly devised a plan to apply for the job without Jacob knowing. If she could convince him that she would be better off in Kansas City than on the farm, he might let her stay and overlook her deviousness.

The car came to an abrupt stop in front of the theater, and Ramona was jolted into reality as Jacob turned to give her the money to buy their tickets while he and Marie parked the car. She opened the door onto the sidewalk under the marquee and was awed by the lights and pictures of the featured stars who were acting in the movie they would soon be enjoying. Ramona stood in line behind several couples whose animated conversations sparked her interest in other activities that would be taking place throughout the summer months, and she made a mental note to share what she had heard with her brother and Marie. It didn't occur to her that Jacob and his girlfriend might want to be by themselves occasionally to develop their relationship to another intimate level and that Marie was growing more and more resentful of the fact that Jacob had not made a commitment to their future as a couple. Ramona's youthful naivety blinded her to the fact that she might be interfering in their lives and could possibly become a wedge in their relationship. At the moment, however, the glittering lights and excitement of the adventure at hand overcame any negative undertones that would surely pop up in the months to come.

Ramona bought the tickets and pushed open the glass front doors that opened into one of the most plush lobbies she had ever seen in any magazine or picture book. The deep red, patterned walls provided a perfect backdrop for the ornate gold filigree light fixtures and the crystal chandeliers. It was as if she was Cinderella and this was part of her magic kingdom. She could not remember when she had been so happy until she heard a familiar voice behind her. Apprehension gripped her heart as she turned and locked eyes with Victor.

"Where is everyone, kid?" was all he could think to say as his date warily took in Ramona's youthful beauty.

Ramona stammered, "They'll be right in after Jacob parks the car!" as she backed away from the well-dressed couple. She kept backing up until she ran into a handsome young man who was ushering for the evening, and as he grabbed her arm to steady her, he flashed a charming smile that made her heart jump. Victor could see the obvious sparks that were flying between the two teenagers, and a jealous rage began to seethe in him until he demanded that the young man return to his job of ushering. A quizzical expression flooded the young man's face, but he realized that he was no match for this twenty-something man and returned to his work station without so much as a backward glance at Ramona.

An unfathomable anger began to take hold of Ramona as she walked right up to Victor and slapped him across the cheek. Afterward, she spotted her brother and Marie and marched behind them into the darkened theater without saying a word. Victor, his date, and a host of other theater patrons stood with open mouths and shocked expressions as the beautiful, blond girl provided them with enough fodder to inspire their gossip sessions for months to come.

With a red face and an injured ego, Victor grabbed his date's arm and ushered her out the front doors of the theater. Inwardly, he was determined to show Ramona that she could not get the best of him, and an ugly plan began to form in his heart. Tonight, however, he was going to show his date how much of a man he really was and spent much more money than he could afford by treating her to an unforgettable night on the town.

After Jacob walked Marie to her door and kissed her sweetly on the lips, he returned to the car, determined to talk to Ramona as soon as they got back to the apartment. However, Ramona's unending chatter about the evening began to wear on his nerves, and his resolve about speaking to her concerning male attraction began to wear thin. By the time they arrived home, Jacob's head was throbbing, and all he wanted to do was retire to his quiet room, slide under the covers, and forget about all the problems that had begun to surface as his sister's visit lengthened. His quiet manner and soft-spoken personality didn't contribute to his ability to hit problems head-on without leaving him depressed and unsure of his effectiveness in solving dilemmas.

He had used his two-week vacation days and was scheduled to return to work the next morning, so he would talk to his sister the next evening after he had time to think about what he was going to say to her. What would Ramona do by herself all day long while he was at work, and what limitations should he impose on her? These were just two of the concerns that floated in and out of his subconscious mind as he fell into a restless sleep.

Monday morning came much too soon, and Jacob reluctantly rolled out of bed as the familiar smell of bacon, eggs, and coffee floated into his room. Ramona had awakened early and cooked Jacob his favorite breakfast, complete with the daily newspaper opened by his plate. Before his sister had a chance to inundate him with endless chatter, he shot her a disapproving look meant to convey the idea that he needed some quiet time to regroup in order to meet the challenge of the day. Ramona reluctantly left Jacob to ponder over the newspaper and retired to her bedroom to decide on a plan of action that would impact her life for at least the next several months.

She waited for her brother to finish his breakfast before she entered the kitchen once again and convinced him that she would be quite satisfied staying in the apartment while he was away at his job. She didn't reveal to him her plans of applying for the job at the cafeteria, but neither did he question her about what she intended to do to fill up her time in the apartment while he was gone. She hugged him as he hesitantly turned to bound down the front steps and drive away toward the brick facade of the factory that provided him with the funds to pay for the apartment. He felt the stress of paying for an apartment that was above his means, but he was convinced that he could afford the rent until his sister left in the fall to return to Springfield.

As soon as Ramona cleaned up the kitchen, she changed into a beige skirt and white cotton blouse. She didn't want to appear too well dressed for the job, but she needed to appear older than fourteen, and that was the only outfit that didn't emphasize her youthfulness. In the year 1924, employers weren't as particular about checking the age of applicants, so it wasn't uncommon for children as young as thirteen to be hired as a sixteen-year-old. Ramona could pass as an eighteen-year-old when she applied her dark red lipstick and pushed her hair into soft waves around her face. She looked at herself in the floor-length mirror and was satisfied that at least she looked old enough to work, whether she was hired or not. She grabbed her purse and without hesitating walked out the front door and down the front steps into her new world where she would be thrust into the responsibilities of adulthood.

When she stepped onto the sidewalk in front of the cafeteria, she was relieved to see the "Help Wanted" sign still posted in the window. Immediately, she felt guilty about the lie she would have to tell in order to apply for the job and nearly turned around to board the next bus that would take her back to the apartment. Instead, she swallowed her guilt and fear and resolutely marched into the cafeteria, where she asked a harried-looking employee the directions to the employment office. She found a shiny mahogany door with the word *manager* etched on a brass plaque at eye level and shyly knocked.

A loud, raspy voice shouted for her to come into the office, and as she slowly pushed the door open, she saw an enormous, bald-headed man sitting behind an incredibly cluttered desk. As if he were late for an appointment, the man quickly asked her what she wanted before he resumed his futile attempts at reducing the tower of paperwork before him. Ramona told him that she wanted to work and that she was qualified to do anything that might be required of her in the cafeteria.

At first glance, my mother obviously didn't impress the manager that she would have the energy nor the desire to tackle the multitude of dirty jobs that were an inevitable part of running a restaurant, so he politely told her that she didn't fit the job description. It wasn't in Ramona's nature to give up easily, so she convinced the corpulent, sweating man to try her out for two weeks. If he wasn't satisfied with her skills, she would accept his decision and continue to search for work elsewhere. He must have recognized the determination in Ramona's voice, or maybe he sensed her urgency to find employment, so he told her to show up for work the next morning at seven o'clock and be ready to put in a full day's work.

Ramona felt like a real adult for the first time, and it was a good feeling. She couldn't wait to tell her brother about her new job and hoped he would be as happy as she was, but she wasn't sure that he would be too excited about her not asking him first. She boarded the first bus that would take her home and ran into the apartment before her brother could call on his lunch break. The phone rang as soon as she shut the front door, and her knees felt like rubber after she hung up because she wasn't ready to tell him what she had done until they sat across from each other at the dinner table.

After kicking off her shoes and putting on one of her sister's aprons that was left behind, she whipped up a delicious meal like the ones their mother served when they grew up on the farm. The aroma of fried chicken, mashed potatoes, and fresh peas filled the air when Jacob opened the front door and walked into the kitchen. A baked apple pie sat on the stove, and his little sister was pouring him a fresh cup of coffee. This was certainly a treat that Jacob hadn't experienced since Bonnie moved out, but something told him there might be an underlying reason for such luscious victuals. It didn't take his sister long to let him know.

As he retreated to the living room to listen to the evening news, Ramona pushed the leather ottoman in front of him and quietly waited until he asked her what was on her mind. The day had been especially hot at the factory, and he was not in any mood to listen to his sister's idle chatter, but he had noticed an especially intense edge in her mannerisms throughout the meal and was curious about what she wanted to discuss with him. As soon as he invited her to share her thoughts with him, the activities of the day spilled out of her mouth as fast as she could share them. She told Jacob that she would help him with the rent and still have enough money left over to buy her own necessities and even be able to save enough to occasionally buy a dress.

Jacob thought about it for a few minutes as Ramona tried to read the thoughts behind his noncommittal facial expressions. Finally, to Ramona's surprise, her brother agreed to let her work throughout the rest of the summer, providing that she tell her employer she would be leaving in the fall. Ramona agreed to his requests but secretly vowed that she would not be returning home at the end of the summer. Jacob also informed her that she would not have to help with the rent but that he would let her buy some of the groceries since money had gotten tighter after Bonnie moved out. He was also glad that he and Marie would have some more time in the early evenings to be together, because he had sensed a growing tension between them. It seemed like years since they had been out on the town together without Ramona, and he yearned for the closeness that they had begun to share before his sister came to live with him.

The alarm clock near Ramona's bed rudely tore her from a deep sleep, and after turning it off, she snuggled under the quilt that her mother had made for Jacob's birthday. The early morning breeze blew against the gauzy curtains, making them billow out like white clouds on a summer's day. As Jacob's fist banged against her door, she remembered that this was the first day of her new job.

She drew her housecoat around her and stumbled into the kitchen to drink a cup of coffee and eat a bowl of hot oatmeal that her brother set before her. After giving her orders about being punctual, he returned to his bathroom to finish getting ready for another day at the factory.

Ramona wasn't sure what to wear but had remembered that the other female employees were wearing jumpers similar to the homemade one she wore on her first day in Kansas City. Luckily, she had washed and ironed it and hung it in the clothes closet for such an occasion as this. She buttoned the white blouse up the front and slipped the jumper over her head. She brushed her hair until it shined like burnished gold and tried to tame the profusion of waves that seemed to multiply overnight. Afterward, she applied a bright red lipstick and a dusting of pink rouge that added at least two more years to her youthful appearance.

Before she left to board the bus, she twirled around to get her brother's opinion on her outfit. Jacob agreed that she had chosen her dress correctly and was secretly relieved to see that the straight lines of the jumper concealed the womanly curves that might encourage unwanted attention from fellow employees or from male customers. He prayed that her health was strong enough to handle a physical job like this and that the Polk work ethic would carry her through whatever she would have to face at her new job. If she decided that this wasn't the job for her after her first day at work, he would understand and encourage her to look for employment at one of the many department stores along Main Street.

It seemed that this was the longest bus ride that Ramona had ever taken. She didn't even come close to understanding what would be required of her and was well aware of the fact that she would probably be the youngest employee at the cafeteria. The only thing she knew was that she was capable of doing a full day's work because she had become accustomed to hard work on the farm and couldn't imagine any job being harder than what she had already done. Her heart began to beat in the same familiar, erratic manner that often accompanied stressful situations, and she fought to keep from passing out. However, she had learned that prayer was the answer to her problems, and after whispering a desperate request to God, her heart miraculously began to beat evenly. She felt fine by the time her bus arrived in front of the Forum Cafeteria.

She stepped off the bus a bit shaken from her experience but had recovered enough to be excited about her new job. The cafeteria would not open for another two hours, so another employee gave her the tour of the kitchen while explaining the duties of each worker. Ramona's responsibilities would be to take charge of the vegetable section of the food line, and this involved making sure that no container would run low and that she would serve the customers in a personable and efficient manner.

This seemed easy enough until the first customers began to move through the line at breakneck speed. Most of them were patient if they had to repeat their order, but she had not been prepared for the few impatient patrons who seemed to enjoy talking down to her as if she were a servant. Some of the other workers noticed her embarrassment and assured her that she was doing a great job. The two twenty-something girls working on both sides of her station occasionally helped her serve the vegetables when she fell too far behind. By the end of the day, however, Ramona was working as quickly as the others on the food line and, after cleaning up her area, left the cafeteria convinced that she would be one of the best workers in the restaurant.

It was getting dark, and she was so tired that she wasn't sure she could mount the steps of the bus. She didn't have to worry about riding the bus on this night, however, because her brother and Marie were waiting in his car in front of the Forum. She was so grateful when she realized she didn't have to ride the bus home that she jumped in the car and gave her brother a giant kiss on his cheek and hugged his girlfriend over the front seat. Jacob was relieved to see that his sister had tackled the day and apparently was satisfied with her job.

Ramona was so tired, in fact, that she fell asleep on the backseat before they arrived at the apartment. Her brother woke her up and made sure that she made it safely in the door before he and Marie left to see the late movie at the Empire Theater. Ramona washed her face and fell into bed as soon as she buttoned up her pajama top and set the clock to wake her up early enough to wash the smell of the cafeteria out of her hair.

She was one of the cafeteria's best workers for the rest of the summer and still had not told her boss that she would be leaving soon. She had helped her brother with the groceries and bought a closet full of new outfits, just as she had planned. She was even able to save enough money to buy presents for her two younger sisters' birthdays and to occasionally buy nylons for her mother. The time to tell her brother that she couldn't bear to return to the farm was approaching quickly, and she prayed he would understand and not send her back.

Jacob had gotten used to having his sister with him and knew how hard it would be to send her back to a situation she dreaded. He had received a sizable raise several months after Bonnie married and wasn't quite as strapped for money as he thought he would be, so he could not in good conscience use that argument as an excuse for sending Ramona back to Springfield. He knew that Mom Polk's heart would be broken if her daughter didn't return to finish her schooling, but he also realized that Ramona's unhappiness would incite their father's anger and she would once again bear the brunt of his insults and discontentment. As the day came near for him to send her back home on the same train she had ridden into town on, Jacob could not be quiet any longer and asked Ramona to sit down and discuss the situation with him over a bowl of popcorn and a cold Coca-Cola.

Ramona's eyes brimmed with tears when he reminded her that it was time to return to Springfield and begin her sophomore year at school. She knew her brother had felt a great responsibility for her and that he would probably be relieved to see her go back home, but she had to try to explain how she felt about returning to such an unhappy situation. He dried her eyes on the corner of a napkin and sat quietly while she poured out her heart. A frantic edge to her voice captured his attention, and he weighed every word carefully as she told about their father's verbal and physical abuse that was mostly directed toward her.

When Jacob and his two older brothers lived on the farm, Jeff consistently whipped all three of them for the slightest infraction of the rules, so he was well aware of his sister's apprehension about returning to such a negative atmosphere. He often wondered why his mother didn't step in and protect her children from their father's frequent rages, but he figured it had something to do with her basic beliefs about the leadership of the man. Nonetheless, the family had suffered from the result of her beliefs, and the only reason the older siblings ever returned for an infrequent visit was because of the gratefulness they felt for her undying determination to provide a good home for them in spite of impossible odds.

Jacob's thoughts were brought back to the moment by Ramona's desperate tone, and he knew he had to make a decision before the day was over so there would be closure to this situation. A plan began to form in his mind about his sister's future, but he wasn't ready to share it with her before he talked to their mother. He assured Ramona that he would think about his decision and give her an answer later that evening, and he convinced her not to worry.

Concern etched his brow as he reached for the phone to call his mother. He was not prepared for her to pick up the phone so quickly, so his hesitation was noted by Ellen before he had a chance to greet her with his usual, "How's it going, Mom?" A silent dread began to attack his mother because she figured that her son's news might send a spear right through her heart, and she wasn't prepared to handle anything else that might impact her life negatively. "Did you call about Ramona?" was all that she could say, and she steeled herself for his answer.

Jacob told her about his conversation with his sister earlier that evening and about how concerned he was over her reluctance to return to the farm. His mother had anguished over the treatment that Ramona had received from her father, but no matter how much she begged her husband to change his attitude toward his second daughter, he seemed more determined to do everything he could to make her life miserable. Ellen had been worried all summer that Jeff would run all of his children off and she would be left to provide all of his needs without the distraction of her family, but she also wanted what was best for each of them. She and Jacob agreed that Ramona could stay in Kansas City if she would continue to study her books each evening and abide by her son's rules, which included attending church and helping her brother with the chores. Ellen even agreed that Ramona should continue working at the cafeteria and that she should learn how to save some of her money instead of spending it on clothes and presents for members of the family.

After some additional discussion about the arrangements, Ellen asked to talk to her daughter. Ramona had been listening to her brother's side of the conversation and reluctantly took the phone to thank her mother for her unselfishness in letting her stay with Jacob. She felt guilty about not being able to help her mother with the work on the farm, but Ellen convinced her that her two younger sisters were getting old enough to carry their weight in the family. Ellen told her daughter how much she was loved and made her promise to visit Springfield as often as her job would allow. Ramona agreed to her mother's wishes and through her silent tears whispered her good-byes before hanging up the phone.

Afterward, both mother and daughter doubled up in grief as each cried a river of tears that flowed out of their broken hearts. Jacob put his arms around his sister and assured her that it wasn't too late to change her mind about returning to her mother, but Ramona had already decided that she couldn't live under her father's roof one more day and set her jaw with a determination to face the future without looking back.

Abigail and Edna embraced their mother as her grief engulfed every muscle in her body, and she nearly collapsed onto the kitchen floor. Jeff walked into the middle of his wife's pain and impatiently demanded to know why she was crying but beyond that never showed any emotion as she sobbed out the decision that had been made about his daughter's future. Anger clouded his eyes as he questioned her reasoning in leaving him out of such an important decision, but Ellen's eyes convinced him that now wasn't the time to be assertive.

He had seen that look only two times before. Once was when she refused to grant him a divorce so that he could marry the widow next door, and the other was when he stayed all night at her farm after Ramona was born. He realized that he played a big part in his daughter's refusal to return to the farm, but he was not prepared to discuss his part of the problem today nor in the near future. He felt no remorse over the loss of another child and even secretly relished the idea of having one less family member to take up space in the house. He had to erase the smile that was threatening to reveal his true feelings until he was safely outside.

Ramona had been his least favorite of the children because she had a determination he couldn't destroy and a will that was so strong since she was a small child that he simply couldn't make her buckle under his ongoing demands. He also had not been successful in robbing her of her zest for life, so he had taken every opportunity to criticize her every move so that at least she wouldn't be happy whenever she was around him. The satisfaction he gained at seeing the hurt in her eyes more than made up for the tension he felt between him and his wife. The anger he still felt toward Ellen's refusal to give him a divorce was a constant thorn in his side, and it had resulted in a bitterness that threatened to smother him whenever he thought about how life might have been with Nell instead of being burdened with what he considered a fanatically religious wife and eight children. No, he wouldn't question his wife's decision to let Ramona stay in Kansas City; instead, he would secretly celebrate the decision and count the years until all of the children would be out of the house. At that time, he would try to find Nell and ask her to leave her husband in order to reestablish a relationship with him and maybe someday marry if he could outlive Ellen.

For the next year, Ramona worked tirelessly at the cafeteria as Jacob continued to date Marie and work at the Nabisco cracker company. They worked out a routine that satisfied them both, and Ramona became the favorite employee at the restaurant. She had a smile for everyone, and the young men began to clamor for her attention. Being away from the farm agreed with her, and she was gaining confidence by the day. She had even been given a raise and was able to open a fairly sizable savings account.

Jacob had driven her to Springfield that Christmas, but beyond that, she had no desire to return to the farm. Instead, she and Jacob had pooled their money after their sisters' school let out that next spring and surprised them with train tickets to visit Kansas City during her week's vacation. Ellen had mixed feelings about letting them venture that far away by themselves, but Jeff assured her that they would be just fine.

Bonnie was able to spend some of her vacation time with them, so the three older siblings arrived early to be there when Edna and Abigail bounced down the train step stool and into their older brother and sisters' world for the next week. They went on picnics, attended the theater, and walked through the zoo at Swope Park. Bonnie and Ramona took their little sisters shopping for new outfits and lunch at the Kresge's soda fountain before they all packed into a picture booth to have their pictures taken. In the evenings, Jacob served his famous popcorn, and they all sat around talking and playing games. The weekend came too fast, and the girls had to board the train heading home on Sunday after church. They had a wonderful time together as a family and hated to break up their fun, but Jacob, Bonnie, and Ramona all had to report for work the next day.

Ramona's heart ached over the way she felt about her family in Springfield and secretly wished that she too could have felt comfortable staying home and finishing high school just as her younger sisters would do. However, that was not the case, and she had resolved herself to the fact that she could never go back to live under Jeff Polk's roof again. If her mother had divorced her father, Ramona felt sure that all of the children would have been much happier, and Jeff would have been out of their lives forever. As it was, she would visit with her sisters as much as she could and plan the rest of her life as a city girl.

Jacob and Marie were no closer to marriage than they were after Ramona moved into her brother's apartment the year before, and Ramona felt that she was partly to blame for her brother's hesitancy. This was not the case, however, because Jacob had a growing addiction to illegal alcohol, and as his relationship with Marie began to cool down, he filled his time drinking with friends from the factory. Marie was devastated and vowed to win him back until she discovered that he had been seeing another woman who periodically hung out with other single guys from Jacob's department. She was a beautiful, long-legged woman who was five years older than Jacob but had much more experience with other men than Jacob had with the opposite sex, and she was looking for a stable man to help her raise her illegitimate daughter.

Ramona did not return home from work each day until late in the evening after the cafeteria closed, so Jacob drank until it was time for them to meet back at the apartment. After a few months of dating Jo, he began inviting her to the apartment, and she frequently spent the night after Ramona dismissed herself and went to bed. The situation became intolerable for Ramona as Jo's visits turned into extended drunken layovers. Jo slowly began to take over the apartment and move more and more of her clothing into her brother's closet. Her young daughter began to spend several nights a week, and Ramona frequently found the child wearing her jewelry and going through her drawers.

After Ramona discussed the situation with Bonnie, they decided to intervene in the situation and remind Jacob that his first responsibility was to his younger sister and not to this woman whose loose morals seemed to be poisoning his mind. Jacob reluctantly agreed to discontinue the frequent overnight visits from his new girlfriend and banned her daughter from Ramona's room. This seemed to work for a while until Jacob began staying out several nights a week, and Ramona's lonely evenings made her situation unbearably unhappy. She was only fifteen years old and had left behind the only friends and family she had known. For the first time she began to wonder if she had done the right thing by leaving the farm.

Bonnie's marriage had begun to deteriorate after the first year because Sam's mother's continual interference into every aspect of their lives began to take its toll on the commitment to each other they had vowed to honor. Finally, after a few more months passed and Sam began to stay out at night using the excuse that he was hanging out with his friends at the local Moose Lodge, Bonnie began to feel uneasy. One night, Sam stayed out much later than usual, and Bonnie asked Ramona to go with her so she could put a piece of bubble gum on his car handle to let him know she had been there. As they arrived at the lodge, they discovered that Sam's car wasn't there, and after marching into the midst of the lodge members and questioning whether or not he had been on the premises, Bonnie discovered that not only had he not been there that evening, he was not even a fellow member.

When Sam sneaked into their apartment late that night, Bonnie was waiting to hear what excuse he would use to explain his whereabouts earlier that evening. He broke down and cried as he told her about his addiction to other women and promised that it would never happen again. The betrayal was so completely unexpected that Bonnie could hardly breathe as she told him to get out and that she never wanted to see him again. He begged for her forgiveness, but as the torrent of tears flowed down her cheeks, she closed her heart against the only true love she had ever felt for any man before or afterward until the day she died.

She asked Jacob if she could move back into the apartment with him and Ramona and help pay for the rent and utilities. Jacob gladly agreed to let her move back in, and the three siblings once again became a family. Bonnie cried nonstop for three months, and Jacob spent more and more time away from home while Ramona continued her search for joy as the lives of her precious brother and sister seemed to be falling apart. It was during this time that Victor began to drop by again to visit with Bonnie.

For the next two years, Ramona spent her days working at the cafeteria and her nights yearning for a life that seemed to be outside of her grasp. She had grown even more beautiful as she approached her seventeenth birthday and had asked Bonnie if she could meet a young man for a date at the Empire Theater. He was an apprentice butcher hired by the cafeteria to supply their meat and had struck up a friendship with Ramona when he delivered their order. He had turned eighteen that fall and had gotten up the nerve to ask Ramona for a date in spite of the fact that he had never asked a girl to go anywhere with him. He bought her a bright red hat and gave it to her the afternoon before their date. He asked her if she would wear it to the theater so he could spot her in the crowd that evening, and she agreed.

After her shift was over, Ramona excitedly ran to the employee restroom at the cafeteria and took off the jumper and white blouse she had worn to work. Hurriedly, she slipped a gray, drop-waist, light wool dress over her head and placed the new red cap over her shiny blond curls. After applying fresh makeup and a squirt of perfume, she fairly skipped out the door and down the sidewalk toward the theater. She did not see her date but wasn't concerned because she had made a point to get there early so they wouldn't be late for the previews.

Fifteen minutes passed, and Ramona began to worry that her date wasn't going to show up. As she turned with a heavy heart to leave and catch the bus heading toward the apartment, she heard her sister shouting her name. Jacob had driven Bonnie to the theater, and from the look on her sister's face, Ramona knew something was terribly wrong. Bonnie told her that after the boy left the cafeteria that afternoon, he had gone back to work to complete an order from one of the local grocery stores. He had accidentally cut a major artery in his groin while slicing the meat that had been ordered, and no one was there to administer medical treatment to stop the blood flow until it was too late. Most of the workers had already clocked out for the night, and the only reason he had been discovered lying on the floor was because his immediate boss saw the light on and had gone to his workstation to turn it off before he left for the weekend.

The young man was so weak that he could hardly talk above a whisper, but he asked if someone would call Bonnie and have her tell Ramona that he was sorry to miss his first date with the most beautiful girl he had ever seen. He died before Jacob could drive them to the hospital, leaving Ramona heartbroken over the unfairness of life. Several days later, the cafeteria was closed so the employees could attend the young man's funeral, and Ramona stood by his grave with the red hat sitting jauntily on her head. She hoped that somehow he could see that she was still waiting for him to take her on their first date.

Bonnie's grief seemed to consume her every waking hour until Ramona and Jacob recommended that she take a trip back to the farm and stay with Ellen and Jeff for at least two weeks while she cleared her head of the confusion that threatened to push her over the edge of sanity. Ellen was excited at the thoughts of having her eldest child with the family for a short time and was confident that the fresh farm air and slower pace of the country would bring her daughter back to her natural penchant for the simpler things in life. Even Jeff was open to the invitation because Bonnie had been his favorite of all the children, and she had visited Springfield so infrequently that he was excited to renew their relationship.

Bonnie didn't feel up to the train ride, so Victor volunteered to drive her in his car, and she accepted his invitation. Her boss agreed that she needed the vacation and encouraged her to enjoy the visit so she could return to his company in a better frame of mind. She was such a good worker that he felt it was in his and the company's best interest to give her space to bounce back from her ordeal without having to worry about losing her job. It was decided that Victor would drive her down to Springfield after he got off of work on Friday afternoon and that he would stay the night at the farm before returning to Kansas City the next day.

Jacob planned to have Jo and her daughter spend the weekend with him at the apartment, so against her better judgment, Ramona asked if she could ride with them and return on the train Sunday evening. Both Victor and Bonnie seemed to relish the idea of having her company, so she packed her valise on Thursday night so she would be ready to go to Springfield when she returned from work the next day. Victor's new Ford sedan was already parked in front of the apartment when she arrived home from work on Friday evening, so she breathlessly ran up the steps and into her bedroom to dress for the trip. She pulled a new light blue angora sweater over her head and buttoned the fashionably short, pleated skirt up the back before she pulled on her new pair of taupe support hose that would conceal the increasingly obvious red veins that had begun to pop out on her lower legs.

The constant lifting of the heavy vegetable containers and the hours of standing behind the food counter were beginning to take their toll on Ramona's already weakened health. Her heart condition had begun to surface more frequently in the form of an irregular cadence that prompted her to lie down in the employees' dining room while the others covered her station. She reaped the kindness that she had shown her fellow workers because they had been glad to cover for her while she recovered from each of her increasingly devastating bouts with a weakened heart muscle. Today, however, she would choose to forget about any problems and enjoy the trip to Springfield and the family that she had left behind.

She slipped on a pair of shiny black pumps and buckled the tiny straps on each side of her feet before brushing her blond curls and tucking them up into the narrowly brimmed, red felt hat. This was the first time she had worn it since the funeral, and she struggled to keep her eyes from brimming with tears. She had toyed with the idea of giving it away, but whenever she put it on, she was reminded that there was someone who thought she was beautiful and that perhaps she would be beautiful to someone else in the future. She applied her new peach-colored lipstick and sprayed some of Bonnie's perfume on her wrists before she opened the door that had protected her from Victor's gaze.

He sat drinking a glass of fresh lemonade and barely moved when Ramona walked into the room with her suitcase. His demeanor exposed his complete lack of interest in her, and she was confused at the changes in his reaction from two years ago when she had slapped him in front of his date at the theater. They exchanged a cordial greeting before he promptly reached for her suitcase to carry it down the stairs and place it in the trunk next to her sister's much bigger valise.

Bonnie joined her at the front door and smiled for the first time since she had discovered Sam's infidelity. The two sisters held hands as they headed toward Victor's freshly waxed Ford sedan and the freedom of the open road. The shiny black paint on the car glowed under the light of the gas street lamps, giving it the appearance of a much more elegant vehicle. At that moment, Ramona felt sure that she knew what Cinderella must have felt when she entered the carriage that would take her to the ball and her future husband. Victor handed each of them a single red rose and eased the car out onto the boulevard and southward toward the farm. Nobody had ever given Ramona a flower, so she was completely taken aback with his unexpected thoughtfulness.

Bonnie fought back silent tears as she remembered the countless number of flower arrangements that Sam had bought for her throughout the first months of their marriage. Immediately, thoughts of her mother-in-law's determination to destroy her marriage flooded her with an anger so deep that she knew it might destroy her if she didn't let it go. She had been a successful accomplice in tearing Bonnie's heart to pieces, but there was some consolation in the fact that Mrs. Vanderson would no longer be an issue in her life.

Lightning lit up the western sky, and Victor sped up as if he wanted to avoid driving through a late fall storm. After an hour of being on the road, the lights of a small town spilled out into the dark sky ahead of them, and Bonnie asked if he would stop at a restaurant so they could get a bite to eat and use the bathroom. None of the three had eaten any supper, so they all agreed to stop at the first decent-looking restaurant.

It was getting late, so most of the better-looking restaurants had already closed. Before they gave up on eating, however, a family diner appeared before them on the side of the road, and they had to make a quick decision to stop or try to find another one in the next town. It was crowded with local townspeople, but Bonnie reminded Ramona and Victor that this was probably their best bet to get a decent meal before arriving in Springfield. Ramona made a mental note to bring food with them the next time they made a road trip so they wouldn't have to stop except to fill the gas tank and use the bathroom.

Victor politely opened each of their doors and helped them step down from the running board as they surveyed the neighborly crowd that was visiting outside in the parking lot. Several of the young farmers stopped talking and stared with their mouths wide open as Ramona and Bonnie walked through the parked trucks. Victor met their hungry eyes with a steely cold gaze that warned them not to say anything about the two beautiful young women who appeared to be his dates for the evening. Admiration replaced desire as their focus turned to Victor, and they wondered how this rather short, well-dressed city slicker could possibly have a date with the two women who had already disappeared through the restaurant doors.

There was a table for two in the front corner next to the window that faced the parking lot, and Victor quickly agreed to pull another chair up so they could be served without waiting for another larger table. He made sure that the young men who were leaning on their farm trucks could see him enjoying the company of his two young companions as he smugly appeared not to notice the attention that was being focused on them. Occasionally, he would lean in toward the two young ladies as if they were sharing a personal secret and revel in the fact that he was the object of a myriad of jealous conversations that were taking place just a few feet outside the window. Ramona and Bonnie were completely unaware of the commotion they had stirred up and continued to enjoy each other's company while keeping up a running conversation about their plans for the next several days.

Ramona had taken off the red hat, and her blond curls bobbed when she shook her head, while her flushed cheeks covered the pallor that had begun to lurk more frequently under her well-applied makeup. Her erratic heartbeat had become a more frequent irritation, but Ramona didn't want to call the doctor until she was ready to accept the fact that there might be something terribly wrong with her physically. Until then, she would conduct her activities as if she were completely healthy and overlook any heart problems until they became an issue in her job.

After eating a hearty country meal of meat, vegetables, and lemon meringue pie, the three travelers left the restaurant to complete the last leg of their journey home. The storm had overtaken them outside of Springfield, but otherwise, their journey had been without incident. Bonnie directed Victor onto the rural farm road that lead to their family's home as he slowed down to avoid splashing the muddy water that had begun to pool in the deep ruts. He wanted to create a good impression with Bonnie and Ramona, so instead of cursing the situation, he kept his thoughts to himself and expertly avoided the jarring potholes. After a few minutes of ear-splitting thunder and crashing raindrops, the storm passed, and the lights of the Polk farmhouse appeared as a beacon to guide them home.

Ellen and Jeff must have been waiting for their headlights because the door flung open before they had a chance to get out of the car. Ramona hung back as Jeff and Ellen both put their arms around Bonnie and held on to her while she released an infinite amount of tears saturated with the frustration and sadness that had become a part of her daily existence. As if his acknowledgment of her presence was an afterthought, Jeff quickly hugged Ramona and introduced himself to the young man who had unselfishly agreed to drive his daughters back to the farm and a much-welcomed visit with the family. Ellen observed Ramona's maturity and grieved over the fact that she had not been with her daughter to enjoy her passage from childhood to the beautiful young woman who was standing before her. She intended to enjoy her two oldest girls for the next several days and concentrate on helping Bonnie overcome the grief that had left her with a broken heart and threatened to rob her of her natural enthusiasm for life.

The warmth from the fireplace felt good as Ramona pulled off her shoes and sat down on the family rocker near the hearth. Her long, shapely legs stretched out from beneath the short, pleated skirt, and Jeff immediately covered her lap with one of Ellen's homemade quilts while making his displeasure known to all. Bonnie realized that her parents resisted any outside worldly influences, so she had picked her wardrobe carefully to avoid any conflict during her visit. Ramona, on the other hand, had been so excited about the idea of taking a road trip that she had forgotten to use wisdom in her choice of fashion. Unfortunately for her, none of the outfits she packed would pass either one of her parents' critical inspection, and if Bonnie wouldn't share her wardrobe, her visit would be miserable.

Victor noticed that Ramona's eyes had filled with tears at the obvious displeasure shown by both of her parents and pulled up a chair to sit beside her to let her know that there was someone in the room who appreciated her and her choice of wardrobe in spite of how the others in the room felt. Ramona quietly asked Victor when he planned to leave the next day and asked if she could leave with him. He assured her that he would stay long enough for her to visit with her sisters and would gladly welcome a passenger to accompany him on his trip home. Gratitude flooded Ramona's heart as she excused herself to get ready for bed.

Ellen followed her to the guest bedroom and visited with her while she changed into her fashionable silk pajamas. Ramona resented her mother's critical eyes as she pulled off her earrings and cleansed her face with a dab of Pond's cold cream. Ellen's religion denounced any type of adornment or makeup, and she cringed at Ramona's determination to break the rules. But she realized that her daughter's soul was filled with the love of the Lord and that her insides were pure even if her outside didn't mirror that fact. As Ramona cleaned the makeup off of her face, Ellen was alarmed at the paleness of her skin and the dark circles that hung beneath her eyes. She wanted to ask her daughter how she was feeling but decided that she wouldn't mention it until the next day after Ramona got a good night's sleep.

Bonnie and her parents talked well into the night and were sleeping late, so the house was quiet when Ramona slipped on her matching silk robe and house shoes and padded to the kitchen, expecting to eat her breakfast in solitude. A movement in the corner of the kitchen caught her off guard, and her heart began its irregular cadence until she realized it was Victor, who had been awake for several hours and had made coffee to take with him while he investigated the barn and fields behind the house. Sleeplessness had always been a problem for Victor, so he usually woke up before sunrise and was dressed before anyone else around him had a chance to calmly roll out of bed, drink their first cup of coffee, and read the newspaper.

Ramona's face flushed with embarrassment when she remembered that she had no makeup on and her hair was a mass of unkempt curls. Victor assured her, however, that she looked great and that she shouldn't have to wear any makeup when she was at her parents' house. He secretly thought that she was the most beautiful woman he had ever seen and wondered if he could ever erase the past and start over again with her on a clean slate. He had long ago forgiven her for slapping him at the theater and even begrudgingly admitted to himself that he might have needed that particular wake-up call even though his ego was bruised for months after his date told the rest of his family what had happened.

"Why don't you walk outside with me, and we'll pet the new calves," was all he could think to say. Ramona was hesitant to walk down the hall and put on some clothes because she might wake up the rest of the family, so she turned down Victor's tempting offer. Victor wasn't easily thwarted, so he grabbed her father's overalls that were hanging in the laundry room and suggested that she pull them up over her pajamas and slip on her mother's rain boots that were sitting on the back steps. It seemed like a crazy thing to do, but suddenly the idea of walking outside in the crisp fall air with a hot cup of coffee in hand appealed to Ramona's sense of adventure, and she grabbed for Jeff's pants without further hesitation. A few minutes later, she and Victor were walking together toward the barn and laughing about how strange she looked in her farm pants, silk pajama top, and shiny black boots.

Ellen had gotten up after the two adventurers had gone outside and was looking at them through the back door. She was usually an excellent judge of character, and she instantly knew that Victor lacked the character to be a good husband and father. She was afraid for her daughter.

She had prayed for her daughters to have a better marriage than she had, but neither one of her eldest seemed destined to have any better family life than they had grown up in. She would pray for their future, but ultimately, it would be up to her children to choose the person they would spend their lives with.

She watched them until a sound behind her brought her back to the reality of cooking breakfast for her family and their guest. She turned and smiled at her oldest daughter as they both reached for a hot cup of coffee and a chair at the kitchen table. Ellen was still a pretty woman, with her black hair cascading down to her waist and her cheeks flushed pink from the heat of the oven. A healthy glow from the summer sun provided a natural makeup that couldn't be bought over a cosmetic counter, and her long, slender fingers toyed with the edge of the checkered tablecloth.

Bonnie had just begun telling her mother about her plans for the future when Edna and Abigail broke into their conversation with a request for pancakes and hot chocolate. Ellen was tempted to tell the girls to cook their own oatmeal while she and Bonnie talked, but Jeff walked in behind them and demanded a breakfast complete with bacon, eggs, and homemade biscuits. He had never been sensitive to the needs of others, so Ellen knew it would do no good to ask him to cook breakfast for himself and the younger girls while she and Bonnie visited. Bonnie jumped up and hugged her father while the younger girls found the mixing bowls and began to stir up a batch of pancakes. Bonnie joined her sisters and prepared the dough for her famous flaky biscuits. It seemed like old times, with everyone lending a helping hand while Jeff checked the fence line that he had repaired the week before.

Jeff reached for his overalls, but Ellen told him to get a clean pair out of the washroom so he wouldn't be upset with Ramona for taking his favorite pair of work pants. After the younger girls finished mixing up their pancake batter, Ellen told them to run out to the barn and tell Ramona and Victor to come in for breakfast. The girls slipped their heavy chenille robes over their pajamas and ran out the back door as they dodged the new family of hungry puppies that were milling around the back steps.

Victor heard the girls shouting their names before Ramona did, and he couldn't help feeling a stab of disappointment because he was enjoying having her by himself. By the time Edna and Abigail had reached the barn, Ramona and Victor were already walking outside clutching their warm coffee mugs and enjoying the crisp fall air. The girls had never seen their big sister in pants, so they found it amusing that Ramona seemed to feel so comfortable in their father's overalls. Ramona introduced Victor as a friend of hers and Bonnie's, and they all four fairly ran back to the house and the warmth of the kitchen.

Jeff threw open the door and shot Ramona a disapproving look when he noticed that she was still wearing her silk pajama top under his overalls. Ramona ignored his obvious displeasure at her appearance and began frying the bacon and eggs as her mother and other sisters set the table, piled the pancakes on a tray, and pulled the flaky biscuits out of the oven. Ellen motioned for everyone to sit down while she set the food on the table. After she made sure that everything was ready to be served, Jeff dutifully said the prayer and ate quietly while the nonstop chatter around him seemed to darken his already surly mood. Their little brother had spent the night with his cousin in town, and Jeff seemed anxious to eat and get on the road before it got any later in the morning.

Several times during the meal, Victor tried to talk about farm life with him, but Jeff wasn't interested in striking up any level of friendship with this outsider. Everyone sighed with relief when he pushed away from the table and announced that he was leaving to get Jack. Victor thanked him for his hospitality as Jeff quickly mumbled his good-byes and turned to leave the kitchen. Ellen couldn't hide the sadness in her eyes as she watched him make his usual escape from their family. It was as if he couldn't stand the joy they shared and had kept all of them at arm's length, except for his young son, who was the result of a surprise late-in-life pregnancy.

When they heard him drive away, everyone jumped up from the table and helped Ellen clean up the kitchen. Victor asked Ellen if there was anything he could fix while he was there because his position of apprentice machinist had given him the skills to be able to repair a variety of broken equipment. There were several jobs that Ellen had asked Jeff to do around the farm, but he never seemed to get around to them. This seemed the perfect time to have her requests honored and also give Victor something to do while she and her girls talked. Victor was relieved to have something to do while he waited for Ramona to finish visiting with her family and hoped that she had not changed her mind about returning with him to Kansas City.

Several hours later, Jeff returned with their little brother after Victor had completed the several repair jobs that Ellen had given him. Jack ran into the house and hugged his mother and sisters before running outside again to feed the puppies. Jeff mumbled something about being tired and retired to his bedroom for the rest of the afternoon.

After eating a quick lunch of cold fried chicken, potato salad, sliced tomatoes, and ample slices of apple pie, Ramona announced that she would be leaving with Victor that evening instead of riding the train back to Kansas City. Disappointment clouded Ellen's face, but Ramona seemed determined to leave earlier than she had originally planned. Her mother suspected that the early departure was a direct result of the discomfort Ramona had felt when she and Jeff showed their disapproval over her choice of clothing. She was not sorry, however, that she had let her daughter know how she felt about the worldliness that seemed to be creeping into all of her older children's lives. It would have broken her heart, however, if she had realized that her middle daughter's faith had begun to be eroded by her legalistic attitude in their relationship. She knew that Ramona had made up her mind to leave shortly after dinner, so she resolutely decided to make the most of the short time they had left and only hope she would be able to show her daughter how much she was loved.

Bonnie, Edna, and Abigail headed toward the kitchen to clean up the dishes while Ellen and Ramona sat in front of the fireplace talking about Ramona's goals for her future. Ellen wanted Ramona to promise that she would study so she could pass her senior tests, but Ramona wasn't sure that she was willing to give the time and effort to receive a piece of paper that gave her the blessing to work when she was already earning her own money. She promised her mother that she would consider granting her this wish, but secretly she knew that she would never give the idea of studying for a high school degree more than a fleeting thought.

After a few more moments of sharing her childhood memories, Jack burst into the room, with Victor trailing behind him, and announced that he had been driving Victor's car down the dirt road in front of their house. Victor had been ready to leave for the past several hours but wanted to make sure that he honored Ramona's request to stay until she was through visiting with her family.

After the girls finished with the dishes, they all joined in the conversation and laughter while Jack tried to impress Victor with his rather extensive collection of toy guns. Time seemed to sit still while everyone shared their dreams and laughed at their mistakes until Jeff interrupted their gaiety by announcing that it was getting late and that if Victor and Ramona wanted to get back to Kansas City before early morning, they should be leaving shortly. Ramona was disappointed that their time together had passed so quickly but was inwardly relieved that she wouldn't have to pass her parents' critical inspection any more that weekend. After she folded her clothes back into the suitcase, she announced to Victor that she was ready to get on the road.

The lights of the Polk farmhouse grew smaller and smaller as they drove down the country road that led them away from the security of Ramona's family and toward the beckoning city lights. The hum of the tires against the pavement lulled Ramona into a deep and troubled sleep, and she didn't wake up until she felt the car slowing down to a stop. She jumped up so fast that she hit her head against the armrest of the door and in her confusion thought that they must have arrived at the apartment. She looked over at Victor and felt a surge of irritation as she noticed the hint of a grin on his lips. Her face grew red from the abrupt blow to her ego as well as from the headache that was beginning to throb with each beat of her heart. Victor asked her if she would like to use the restroom while he gassed up the car, and she abruptly said yes with a hint of annoyance in her voice. She shoved her feet into her summer wedges and walked unsteadily through the loose gravel toward a most welcomed oasis.

When she opened the door to the restroom and turned on the light, the cockroaches scurried to hide in every crack of the bathroom floor, and she let out a terrified scream. Victor stopped pumping gas and ran to find out what prompted his beautiful passenger to let out that bloodcurdling scream. He found Ramona clutching her breast outside of the closed door and pointing toward the bathroom. He flung open the door, half expecting to see a dead body or a snake curled up inside the toilet bowl, but instead was relieved to see an army of frightened roaches trying to scurry to safety.

He smashed as many as he could and asked Ramona if

she would be more comfortable waiting for another filing station that might have cleaner bathrooms. The offer was tempting, but Ramona wanted to get home before too much later, so she squeamishly shut the door and wiped the toilet seat with paper before she reluctantly used the bathroom. Afterward, she pulled her socks up and her skirt down as she squinted her eyes as small as she could get them so she wouldn't have to see the dead bodies of the bugs that littered the floor around her feet.

Adding insult to injury, Victor was furious when Ramona returned to the car because he had forgotten to turn the gas flow off before coming to her aid and was acting like it was her fault that gas had been spewing out of the tank and onto the ground for at least five minutes. Fortunately, another customer had driven up and turned it off before any more damage had been done to his budget. Consequently, his gas bill was twice as much as it would have been otherwise, and he had little money left for the rest of the week. Ramona noticed his sullenness and offered him the money she would have had to pay for a train ticket. He was tempted but had to remind himself that Ramona wasn't just some trollop he was used to dating and wanted to impress her with his chivalry. He gallantly said no to her generous offer, and together, they drove out onto the highway that would take them home.

Ramona asked him about his family since he had met all of hers, and she sensed an undercurrent of sadness as he asked, "What would you like to know?" Ramona didn't know where to begin, so she asked about his mother and how she became an owner of a boardinghouse. Slowly,

Victor began to tell her about how his mother moved to Kansas City with his littlest sister and his stepfather when he was a small child, leaving him with his aunt and uncle in Appleton City, Missouri. He told her how hard it had been to grow up in such an impoverished situation without a mother or father but that he had somehow lived through those times and was doing well in his apprentice position with a local machine shop.

Even as he spoke about his mother leaving him at such an impressionable age, Ramona sensed that there was no animosity in Victor toward her. In fact, he projected a loyalty toward her that seemed to override any anger that he could have harbored against her under the circumstances. Ramona began to sense that there were more positive character traits under the surface of the young man than he was willing to share or perhaps even realize. The wall of protection she had built between her and Victor began to weaken as he told her about living with his uncle and how he had never been able to attend school past the eighth grade.

As fortune would have it, however, Uncle Harry was a barber with a rather impressive list of prosperous clients who were willing to help him out in various situations. When his nephew Victor needed a job, he asked one of his clients who owned a machine shop if his nephew could be hired as an apprentice machinist, and he agreed to let him try in return for a year's worth of free haircuts. My father, in turn, promised Uncle Harry that he would pay for their utilities for the next year, and everyone was happy with the deal. It turned out that Victor was a natural at working the math that was necessary to become a precision tool and dye maker and caught on to the business of being an expert machinist much quicker than anyone thought he would. His reputation soon spread to the other companies, and in spite of his volatile temper, he was able to earn decent money as a machinist for the rest of his working life.

Time passed swiftly as Ramona and Victor visited and laughed at his witty humor. By the time they pulled in front of the apartment, Ramona had lost all of the apprehension she formerly felt toward Victor and exchanged an affectionate hug with him before they both said their goodnights. Victor wanted to kiss Ramona and tell her what a good time he had, but he knew that he had to take it slowly with her this time or he would run her off again—maybe for good this time. He was tired, but his feet barely hit the steps as she shut the door behind her because Ramona said he could call her that week and take her to see a picture at the Empire Theater. Life had suddenly lost its gloom because he felt that the sun had finally begun to shine on him and his future.

For as long as he could remember, he had never left a date with this feeling of joy—and he didn't even kiss her. That's the part he wouldn't tell his uncle because Harry just wouldn't understand why his nephew didn't demand some sort of affection more than a hug. His own associations with women had always been filled with sex and lewd passion, so he wouldn't understand how anyone would want to wait in the pursuing of self-gratifying lust.

Victor hoped that his uncle would be in bed when he got to the house, but in case he wasn't, he would point out how late it was and that he had to get up early to go to work. His uncle was off on Mondays, so he usually entertained one of his dates for the evening at the house and didn't pay much attention to his nephew. Victor hoped that this would be the case tonight. Uncle Harry didn't own a car because he considered it an inconvenience when he could hail a taxi to take him anywhere he wanted to go or use his nephew's automobile if he wanted to impress a date. Tonight, he must have chosen to stay at one of his girlfriend's abodes because the apartment was quiet and there were no lights on in any of the rooms.

Victor sighed a sigh of relief because he often came home to drunken orgies and half-naked women who pawed over him as soon as he tried to escape to his own bedroom. Most of the time, the midnight parties were repugnant to him, but occasionally he was drawn into the activities by an especially attractive visitor and often woke up the next morning after one of those trysts wondering if this was all there was to life as the stranger who shared his bed moaned from a hangover of monstrous proportions. Tonight, he slipped between the sheets thinking about how good Ramona made him feel when he was around her and how he couldn't wait to see her again. He knew he had to be extremely careful about asking her for dates because not only did her brother mistrust his motives, but Ramona was as jumpy as a cat around him. He couldn't wait to have sex with her, but he was willing to give her enough time to feel comfortable around him before he tried to arouse passion within her by using the techniques he had mastered from an early age.

Victor's sleep was more peaceful than any he could ever remember, and he awoke the next day refreshed and ready to embark upon a plan that would convince Ramona that he was the right guy for her. He whistled as he gulped down a black cup of coffee and dressed for work. His boss was impressed with the speed at which he learned how to use the machinery in the shop and was ready to give him some rather complicated assignments to complete if Victor could control his emotions.

Victor was a hard worker, but it was becoming increasingly apparent to everyone working around him that he was an incredibly angry man. He would not socialize with any of the men at break time and became hostile when anyone questioned the quality of his work. After several months of dealing with his surly attitude, the man who agreed to mentor him made an appointment to have Uncle Harry cut his hair. He told Victor's uncle that he could not continue letting Victor work at the shop if he didn't control himself and lighten up around the other men. Several of the machinists had voiced their complaints against Victor and threatened to find work at other machine shops if something wasn't done to regain the pleasant atmosphere that prevailed at the shop before Victor came. Ed, Victor's boss, was assured by Uncle Harry that his nephew would present a more pleasant attitude the next time the doors opened for business, or he would kick him out of his apartment. Apparently, Victor believed Uncle Harry because his attitude was much better after their conversation, and he went on to complete his training without a hitch.

Victor would be starting a new job at a shop near

Ramona's apartment in a few weeks, and he could drop by to visit with Bonnie and Ramona on his way home as often as he wished because Bonnie saw him as a friend in whom she could confide. He could keep an eye on Ramona's activities while he and Bonnie visited about her broken marriage and future plans. Jacob hardly ever stayed at the apartment after Bonnie moved back in because he had set up housekeeping with Jo and her daughter. He had gotten tired of the responsibilities of having a teenager under his roof, so he was happy to let Bonnie have his job. He did not realize that Ramona was old enough to make many of her own decisions because she had turned seventeen in November and had learned to be responsible with her finances for the past three years.

Ramona had not developed a social life because there never seemed to be enough time to date after working her shift at the cafeteria. She was too tired after work to do anything but come home and fall on the divan after eating a light meal and listening to the radio before falling asleep by nine o'clock each night. On the weekends, she had to wash her uniforms, shop for food with Bonnie, and attend church services on Sunday. There never seemed to be enough time to pursue friends her own age, and she didn't know where to find any except at church.

Most of the girls her age were just graduating from high school, and she had nothing in common with any of them. The boys were immature and looked down on Ramona because she didn't have a high school education and did not live with her parents. It seemed inevitable that she would end up with someone like Victor because she didn't seem to fit into any type of social situation that was common to others her age, and she was lonely. She didn't realize that she was stunning in appearance and pleasant in nature and could have dated many men of different ages and occupations. Eventually, she settled for less when she married Victor because she felt that her choices were limited, and she didn't want to face old age without a husband and family.

Victor made it a habit of stopping by Bonnie and Ramona's apartment several times a week until both of them grew quite comfortable when he came around. Sometimes he would bring them their meal from a local restaurant, and other times he would ask them if they would like to accompany him to a local bistro where they could sit outside and enjoy the summer nights as they ate under the stars. On one of those visits, he introduced Bonnie to a rather shifty-looking man he had met through his uncle Harry. He was older but was well-built and carried himself with self-confidence. Soon, both Victor and Clem were visiting with the sisters and even began double dating occasionally.

Bonnie's grief was still an issue in her life, and she seemed blinded by it. Clem would not have been a man she would have carried on a lengthy conversation with under normal circumstances, but because of her brokenness, she had become vulnerable to his advances. In no time, Bonnie was seriously dating Clem, and after a weekend of visiting with his family in Arkansas, she agreed to marry him and move to a small town across the southern border of Missouri.

Victor continued to visit with Ramona at the apartment

after Bonnie moved away, and as nature took its course, their intimacy paved the course for their marriage on Ramona's eighteenth birthday. The morning was darkly threatening, with reports of snow and sleet scheduled for later on in the afternoon, and Ramona felt an ominous tension at the prospect of becoming Mrs. Victor Baxter. She turned over, covered her head with her pillow, and did something she had not done for a very long time—she prayed! It felt good to talk to God about her dilemma, but she could not hear God's voice like she could as a child when she knelt beside her bed in the loft of the old farmhouse.

Her heart began its familiar irregular cadence, and she felt like she was being strangled. Her head felt light as she began to feel herself falling into a dark tunnel. Suddenly, she felt a sweet peace as she drifted into unconsciousness and became willing to venture into the next life without any fear of leaving behind any worldly concerns. Her surroundings came into focus, however, when the telephone by her bed shocked her back to reality and the gravity of her situation. When she realized that the voice on the other end of the line was that of her mother's, relief flooded her like a refreshing wind, and she began to cry until her body heaved with each new sob.

Ellen's concern for her daughter's welfare had piqued in the last several weeks, and something in her spirit had prompted her to call Ramona. She had a feeling that Victor was at the center of her daughter's increasing unhappiness, but she felt that she would be intruding in their lives if she told Ramona how she felt about Victor and his family. Ramona had not informed anyone in the family that she and Victor had planned to get married at the justice of the peace that afternoon because she knew in her heart that no one would be willing to give their blessing on this marriage. If her mother knew the things that Victor had talked her into doing before they made a formal commitment to one another, she might possibly be disowned, and she couldn't face that possibility.

Ramona shared with her mother about her worsening heart condition, and Ellen prayed for her over the phone. But Ramona did not reveal any details about her relationship, even though she felt like she was betraying her mother's confidence by keeping her impending marriage a secret. She had prayed many times that she would have the nerve to tell Victor that she would like to put their marriage off until a later time, but she was sure that in his anger he would make her suffer for this decision. Reluctantly, she thanked her mother for her prayers and assured her that she would take better care of herself.

Ellen hung up the phone with a heavy heart and an unsettled spirit. Somehow, she knew that her daughter was in grave danger from some unexplainable source, and she had to put her in God's hands because she knew Ramona was hiding a terrible secret from her. She couldn't imagine what it was. If she only knew that her daughter's impending marriage was going to place her into the midst of one of the most irreverent families imaginable, she would not be able to handle the implications of that reality. Perhaps she could have talked Ramona out of marrying Victor if she realized how close they were to becoming husband and wife.

By the time Victor appeared at her front door to usher

her to his waiting automobile and her date with destiny, Ramona had pulled herself together and was even able to manage a weak smile as she resolutely walked beside him to begin their journey together as man and wife. They had invited another couple from the apartment above to be their witnesses at their marriage ceremony, and they were happily chatting in the backseat as Victor opened the door for his future bride to sit beside him in the front.

Ramona had met Mable several months before when she appeared at the front door asking for a cup of flour to make her husband a birthday cake. They instantly liked each other's personalities, and she became Ramona's first real friend since she left Springfield. Her husband, Ben, was a happy-go-lucky sort who seemed to have a constant grin on his ruddy face, and he was agreeable to letting his wife visit with Ramona whenever she wanted. Ramona and Mable talked for hours about their expectations in life, but Ramona never let her friend know the doubts she felt about marrying Victor. Somehow, she knew that if Mable knew about her true feelings, she would talk her out of getting married, and she wasn't strong enough to face the consequences of those decisions. Her life had spun out of control; she was caught on a treadmill that was leading her down a path to destruction, and she knew it. She felt totally unable to stop fate and step off of that self-destructive path that was leading her toward a future filled with betrayal, unhappiness, and poor health.

Their car pulled in front of a charming, two-story Victorian house with the name of a justice of the peace engraved on a brass plate attached to one of the pillars that stood on either side of the red brick steps. Mable pinned a corsage of white rosebuds onto the lapel of Ramona's blue silk suit, and they all walked into the waiting room of the house where the weddings took place. The justice appeared as soon as the foursome entered his domain and asked Victor if he had their marriage license. Victor produced the document, and the wedding vows were exchanged. Almost before Ramona had a chance to consider the implications of her promise to be faithful to Victor for the rest of her life, the ceremony was over, and the justice pronounced them man and wife. Victor kissed his bride and shook hands with Ben before they signed the license and turned to leave the charming house.

After a short dinner with their friends, Victor and Ramona drove to a motel in the Ozarks to spend their first night as man and wife in the Boston Mountains. Reality about her situation set in when she realized that her new husband had not left his old ways behind. She had slept later than usual and awoke to find Victor gone. Alarmed, she quickly dressed and made her way to the restaurant next door, where she found him laughing and flirting with the young waitress who was sitting at his table. When she sat down beside him, she could sense that he felt she was an intruder in a situation in which she wasn't wanted, so she cleared her voice and excused herself to go back to the room.

With tears in her eyes, she fairly ran back to the room and began to dress for the trip home when Victor threw open the door and demanded to know why she had left so abruptly. Ramona said, "If you don't know, then I can't explain it to you." Secretly, she realized that this type of behavior would be an issue in their marriage for the rest of their lives, and she was right. Sorrow filled her heart when the full impact of her situation began to sink in, and she was ready to cut their "honeymoon" short and return to the city. Victor didn't want to spend money on another night's stay at the motel, so he agreed to drive his new bride back to the apartment.

They had decided to stay in the building where Ramona lived for the past four years but agreed to rent a smaller apartment with two bedrooms instead of three. As they drove up in front of the apartment building, Ramona felt a sense of peace because the familiarity of the situation offset the growing doubts she was harboring in her heart.

After their first year of marriage, the depression hit with a ferocity, and Victor was out of work for a year. He demanded that Ramona apply for a job at the meatpacking plant in spite of her weakening heart condition so she could make more money. They had saved enough of their income to remain in the apartments for at least another six months, but Victor wanted to make sure they had enough money saved to offset any emergency that might occur. Ramona reluctantly told her friends at the cafeteria that she would be leaving them and with a heavy heart started working in the frozen food section of the plant. It was here that she met the young man who unknowingly stole her heart, and she secretly kept his memory safely tucked away until she told me about him two months before she died at the age of eighty-six. Perhaps he fulfilled an unattainable dream she had about finding true love because she had not found even a semblance of an abiding love between herself and Victor no matter how hard she tried.

The next fifty years passed quickly as Ramona held their family together with determination and strong faith. Their three children grew up and started their own lives, leaving Victor and Ramona alone once again to face a hollow marriage filled with unhappy memories. They decided to stay together because of financial reasons, but it was Ramona who remained faithful to her vows and continued to be the Proverbs wife who took care of Victor as he wasted away from the ravages of cancer that eventually ended his life.

The viewing was nearly over, and I could hardly wait to hunt for a bathroom. I looked over at my mother to see if she was ready to leave because I wanted her to accompany me in my search for relief. She cordially dismissed herself from the presence of my father and his youthful sidekick and grabbed hold of my arm as we undertook our quest. After stumbling into several other viewing rooms in which solemn-looking cadavers lay peacefully in their final beds, we found an official-looking man who kindly led us to our destination without another hitch. I would have been afraid to wander around a funeral parlor on my own, but with my mother close beside me, I felt the same confidence that I had always felt as a child when she assured me that everything was going to be all right as long as I depended on God to give me peace.

We had not been gone long when we heard the clicking of shoes on the tile floor outside of the bathroom door. Just as Mother and I were washing our hands, Aunt Stella flung open the door and demanded that we return to Grandmother's Gus's viewing room immediately because the viewing wasn't officially over. Surprised and embarrassed over our mistake, we hurried back to our seats as quickly as we could and settled ourselves while angry eyes and pursed lips greeted our untimely intrusion.

Chapter Six

An operatic, well-trained voice singing "Ave Maria" brought me back to my grandmother's viewing. I was surprised that my cousin was singing today instead of tomorrow at Gus's funeral, but someone said she wanted to give her grandmother a special tribute in remembrance for all she had done for her. My cousin was treated differently from us throughout our childhood years, and she was truly thankful that my grandmother had been there for her when her own mother and father were unable to assume their role of parents because of their frequent alcoholic binges. Candace was truly the apple of my grandmother's and Aunt Stella's eyes because they had assumed much of the responsibility for raising her. My brothers and I, on the other hand, were frequently thrust upon Grandmother Gus, and she wasn't happy with the intrusion into her lifestyle, which consisted of activities devoid of any redeeming value.

My cousin was fifteen years older than me and was

a senior in high school by the time I was old enough to remember much about her. I do remember how her hair shined like burnished brass as I sat on her bed watching her brush her thick mass of curls. My brothers and I weren't allowed to enter her bedroom, but my cousin would occasionally ask me to come in and sit on her bed when she saw me walking down the hall to the bedroom reserved for visitors of boarders. The first time I saw her room, I was completely in awe over the opulence of the décor.

Her door was ajar, and I peeked in to see if she was there. To my complete surprise, I felt that I had walked into the bedroom of a princess. The canopy on her four-poster bed was gathered at each end by a cluster of rosebuds, and the silk, mint green and pink bedspread cascaded over the edges of the bed and brushed against shiny wood floors covered with fluffy, white throw rugs. An enormous collection of stuffed animals covered her pillows, and a brass mermaid stared into a blue globe on the lamp next to her bed. Pictures of famous opera singers graced her walls, and white lace curtains gracefully hung down over her windows.

On that particular evening, a ceramic Christmas tree with real electric lights sat in front of one of her windows. A thin sheet of ice had coated the windowpanes, creating a tapestry of color and design that was interrupted periodically by water droplets warmed by the new steam heaters standing at attention under each window. My mother was in the hospital again, and I yearned for my own Christmas tree and my own presents. The overpowering beauty of the scene completely took away any fear of reprisal for entering taboo territory, and I was compelled to touch a delicate branch of that work of art.

Just as my tiny finger touched the smooth glass of the tree, a stabbing fear took hold of my body as I saw my grandmother's reflection in the window. She was stealthily tiptoeing up behind me, ready to pounce on my fragile body and whip me with a belt that normally hung on her bedroom door. Her mouth was pursed into a thin line, and I thought I saw hate in her eyes as she grabbed my arm and hit my bare legs with the belt. I knew it would do no good to scream out for help, so I bit my lip and only screamed out at each hit of the leather strap. She continued to beat my legs until my cousin appeared in the doorway with a quizzical look on her face.

My grandmother said, "I caught Caryn trying to unscrew the lights on your tree after I told her not to come in here." I wanted to shout out that she was telling a lie, but I knew I would be placing myself in more danger if I told the truth. My cousin seemed to have a gentle heart and told my grandmother that I could stay in her room and visit with her until she was ready to leave on a date with her future husband.

Tears of pain and fear were coursing down my cheeks as I glanced up at my grandmother's face. A warning look in her eyes let me know that I had better not tell my cousin anything other than what was said or I would be punished again later. I suppose my brothers had already gone to bed because I don't remember them being at Grandmother's house that night. Perhaps my father sent me to keep my grandmother company because he knew that after her visitors on the porch left each evening, she would be alone in the house except for the occasional boarder who would stop by and chat with her before they went to their room for the night. Sometimes I think that maybe he thought I might bring the same joy to her that my cousin did, but that never happened.

My mother's Christian values had become a part of my upbringing in spite of my father's resistance to anything that had to do with her faith, and those values always seemed to increase my grandmother's feelings of hostility toward me. She was determined that no one would share my cousin's place of importance in her heart or her house. She also didn't want to be saddled with my brothers and me in case my mother died before we were grown, so she kept an emotional distance as well as a physical distance unless she was "punishing" us.

My cousin had begun to attend church with her boyfriend's parents several years before, and I felt a kinship with her because she was like my mother and her friends at Bible study. Her eyes were kind when she wiped my tears dry that night, and she even let me try on one of her beautiful hairpieces that she wore when she sang opera in the outdoor theater at Truman Park. My tears soon turned to smiles as she dabbed some of her makeup on my face and told me that she was glad I was her cousin. I don't remember her telling me that I could come into her room whenever I wanted, but I somehow realized that unless she was busy, I would always be welcome to come in and visit her.

Later, after she left with her boyfriend, I ran to my room and jumped into my bed before my grandmother had a chance to accuse me of something else I didn't do. I heard her footsteps in front of my door during the night, but they turned and went back down the hall toward her own bedroom when she saw that there was no light on in my room. After each of these especially traumatic events, my fear of her became so penetrating that my asthma attacks began to surface even at the mention of having to visit her house.

There was an evil aura surrounding her and most of the people who hung around to drink her homemade liquor. I don't remember her cooking anything except enormous roasts surrounded with carrots and potatoes, and that was on the weekends. She pieced on the meat throughout the week and made sandwiches out of other various cuts of meats that were brought to her from the restaurant at the stockyards by my aunt Stella. She also kept cherry-filled rolls covered with white icing in the drawer of her white metal kitchen cabinet, and when my brothers and I pulled the drawer out to satisfy our own sweet tooth, cockroaches scattered in all directions. Grandmother never wrapped the rolls in any waxed paper because it apparently didn't bother her that she shared her stash of sweets with an army of roaches. Maybe it was her way of not having to share with us because she knew we would never open that drawer again after we discovered the secret of the metal cabinet.

I'm sure the house seldom got a real cleaning because I never saw my grandmother lift a finger to clean anything except for the time when I caught her sweeping dirt under her living room rug. When she discovered that I was staring at her, she threatened to hit me with the broom, and I ran for dear life. Spiders were a problem in the dark corners of her baseboards, and gnats always seemed to be flying around in her kitchen. My cousin's room seemed to be the only truly clean room in the house, and I suspect that she was the one responsible for keeping it that way. It was obvious that my aunt and grandmother didn't hold back on showering her with expensive clothing and furniture for her room, but she never lost her humble attitude and passion for practicing her opera until she fine-tuned her skills.

Aunt Stella had paid for Candace to attend the Kansas City Conservatory of Music where she honed her skills and was asked to accompany other fine musicians on their journeys throughout the world of the arts. Aunt Stella also paid for Candace's taxi ride across town each day in order for her to be able to attend classes. She made many friends at the Conservatory who thought she was rich because she seemed cultured and wore the latest styles straight from the most up-to-date catalogues. They wondered why she never invited any of them to her home, but this just added to the mysterious quality of Candace's personality, and she was accepted by even the most society-minded families in the Kansas City area. Her shiny bronze-colored curls encircled her pleasant features, and she sang herself straight into the hearts of many hopeful young suitors. Their plans to date this charming young singer were soon dashed, however, after they found out that her heart had already been claimed by the young man she had known since her thirteenth birthday and would eventually marry. As far as I know, Candace never dated anyone seriously besides her future husband, and their love for one another seemed to grow deeper with the passing of the years.

I'm not sure she ever knew that she was one of my idols, and perhaps I should have told many years ago. Her marriage to the young man who later became a dentist with my aunt's financial help seemed to be happy and fulfilling for her whole family. My grandmother was unable to impart her own hollow values upon her favorite niece, and that in itself was a miracle because Candace spent as much time with her as she did with her own mother and father.

As my cousin finished singing for our grandmother, there was not a dry eye in the room. Her heartfelt emotions for my grandmother reached out and touched everyone there. Afterward, she sat down in the front row on the other side of my mother and quietly stared at the still body in the casket. Her husband didn't move from his chair to join her but instead offered the seat next to him to my uncle Danny, who had just returned from the outside door where he had been sitting in his Cadillac downing a considerable amount of whiskey. They did not speak a word to each other as Uncle Dan plopped down on the waiting chair. Instead, they nodded a silent greeting before they resumed their people-watching from their rather safe distance.

Chapter Seven

Loud sobbing interrupted the ambiance of the moment, and everyone strained to see who was responsible for that display of raw emotion. There, standing among the floral sprays at the back of the casket, was my aunt Stella. Rivulets of tears were coursing down her cheeks as she relived the years of memories as a drowning man might view his life before death overtakes his thoughts and he starts his destination on a path to eternity. Every few minutes, she would touch my grandmother's cheek or pat her folded hands and cry harder. It was as though she was still trying to find the love that she had strived for all her adult life.

The coldness emanating from the lifeless corpse was not much unlike the emotions she felt when her mother was alive. She and her siblings had one thing in common, and that was to pretend that they had close family ties with their mother. She had been especially diligent throughout the years to provide Gus with her material needs in order that she might be able to cultivate some sort of relationship that could possibly spring from a thankful heart. Perhaps that was part of the reason Gus had been fairly nurturing to my cousin. My grandmother's decision to have my aunt's tubes tied at the early age of fifteen did not seem to deter Stella from seeking her mother's approval even when she longed for children after her marriage to Uncle Danny.

My aunt had moved to Kansas City several years before my father left Appleton City and was allowed to move in with Ed and Gus after her stepfather agreed to let her make the move in return for her agreement to pay rent. She rarely stayed at the house, and when she did, she brought an innumerable number of men to her room to spend a night of wanton pleasure with her mother's blessing. As long as Ed received his check at the beginning of each month, he and Gus didn't seem to care what Stella did. In fact, several of the men who frequented her daughter's bed became quite good friends with Gus and her husband, and it was with their help that my grandmother and aunt were able to meet several prominent city officials who were willing to give advice on legal issues that periodically popped up.

My aunt was short and thick-bodied like her mother, but she had a distinctly Native American look about her. She told us that she had been introduced to her natural grandmother only once, and she was as dark as any Negro she had ever seen except that she was a full-blooded Apache Indian. It seemed that my grandmother had been especially close with a young Indian who moved into Rich Hill for a short while before he quietly disappeared into the night, leaving Gus pregnant with his child. He often wore his full Indian regalia while moving about town, and I'm sure her husband wouldn't have had any trouble holding a kangaroo court with several of his cronies and carrying out their own style of final judgment on the amorous Indian lad had he stuck around.

My aunt told us children many times throughout our childhood that she was an Indian princess and qualified for a government check as such if she so chose, but that was the extent of her divulgence of any further information about her Native American lineage. Only when she and my father argued did the topic come up, and that was when he called her the "Chief." Years later, as my younger brother and I visited her grave, we were shocked to see a granite headstone next to her and my uncle Danny's plot engraved with the family name of the young man who supposedly was her father. We felt that there was much more to that story than we would ever find out, but my grandmother and aunt were successful in taking most of those secrets with them to the grave.

My aunt had an incredibly determined nature and a keen business sense, at least in areas where she stood to make a sizable amount of money. She had made contacts with many of the influential businessmen of the city and wasn't above using whatever means she found at her disposal to get her way. She was ruthless in her personal dealings as well as in business matters, and most of the people who grew to know her realized that it might be personally dangerous for them to disagree with her when her mind was set. She was a hard worker and was basically the breadwinner as my uncle became more and more mentally challenged from his constant drinking binges.

After I graduated from high school, I agreed to work for a week in her cigar stand so she could escape a few days from behind the counter. I had to wake up at three o'clock in the morning in order to be at the hotel by 4:30 a.m. and be ready for the cowboys as they strode through on their way to the stockyards. I ate a candy bar once in a while as the mornings wore on, and apparently, one of her admirers told her that I had stolen her candy and had not placed the appropriate money in the cash register to repay her. I believed that since I was her niece and was not accepting full pay for doing the job, she wouldn't care if I ate an occasional candy morsel. This was not the case, however, and after she berated me for stealing from her, she took the amount of the cost of the bars out of my check for that week. Obviously, that was the last time I ever worked for her, and the realization of just how little I meant to her once again hit me full force in the face.

My relationship with her was very confusing as a child because she could be very generous on one hand and incredibly cruel on the other. She bought me an enormous bottle of Chanel No 5 when I was in elementary school and occasionally gave my mother money to buy me clothes from several of the most expensive department stores in Kansas City. Many times, she would ask me what I would like from her shelves when my family visited her and Uncle Dan at their lakeside home and then turn around and demand that I return my treasure to her before we left for the evening.

She paid for my brothers and I to take swimming lessons so we could swim in the lake and let us drink soft drinks from their bar. She bought us ice skates so we could skate in front of their house in the winter and let my brothers and I help decorate their party barge for the Fourth of July each summer. Occasionally, I was allowed to sunbathe on the roof of their boat dock as long as I didn't bring any friends with me to enjoy the sunshine. Also, my uncle Danny agreed to let me ride on his party barge if there was room for me to sit between the other passengers who always seemed to stand in line for a ride around the cove with a glass of my uncle's favorite whiskey held firmly in their hands. My mother and father didn't drink, so our exposure to their style of life was understandably regulated, and therefore, we weren't subjected to the frequent brawls and other activities that are commonly associated with drunkenness. I believe that both my aunt and uncle were lonely and longed for a family of their own, and because of this, they were willing to supply whatever amount of food and alcohol that was necessary to keep company around them most every night.

A certain Fourth of July stands out in my mind when I think of their infamous parties. I was eight years old, and we had just returned from California, where my family was fortunate to have lived down the street from my mother's sisters and their families for three years. My father was accused of having an affair with another man's wife, and we were unceremoniously torn away from the part of the family that I continue to have fond memories of to this day. My brothers and I had established strong bonds with our cousins and were forced to begin the process of readjusting to the fact that we were once again being thrust into the middle of my father's family.

My mother had made potato salad and baked beans to take to the lake for a day of swimming and fireworks, but the joy of that occasion was cut short by a brawl that took place between the next-door neighbors and my aunt's guests. My younger brother had lit a cherry bomb and rolled it down the sidewalk toward the lake just as the neighbor's blind cocker spaniel ran over to take a leak on my uncle's lawn. The sound of the burning wick of the firecracker must have piqued his curiosity because he ran toward the small red bomb just as it blew up in his face. His howls of pain enraged the neighbors and their visitors, and they charged onto to my aunt and uncle's lawn, all the while cursing my brother for hurting their dog. It did not seem to occur to them in their drunken state that their dog wandered into my aunt's territory, and they weren't prepared for the melee that followed.

My aunt took off her shoe and proceeded to beat the leader of their pack on the head while my uncle landed a few of his famous punches on their teenage son's chin. Everyone on their side of the lake seemed to get into the act as fists flew and curse words turned the air blue. I didn't know what to do as my mother clutched her breast and my brothers hid in the bar downstairs, so I nervously giggled at what I perceived was a ridiculous situation. My aunt stopped her fist in mid-air and stomped toward me with fire in her eyes as I hid behind my mother for protection.

She seemed to blame this whole battle on my brothers and me and was angry that I was laughing at her dilemma.

Later, as guests from both parties licked their wounds and settled in for the night, my mother suggested that my father take us home before my aunt could direct any more of her displaced anger toward us three children. We never ate the food that had been prepared for that afternoon because my uncle neglected to cook the meat after the brawl, and my mother didn't feel comfortable feeding our family the food she had brought when no one else was eating.

Fourth of July was a day full of swimming, laughter, and drunkenness throughout my childhood. But even through the rather ribald festivities, I sensed a real respect for the American flag and all that it represents. It was easy to share my aunt and uncle's sense of patriotism when their flagpole was at full mast and at least a hundred small flags dotted the edge of their lawn. Their visitors saluted the flag periodically, and my aunt would usually give out various patriotic pins that lit up, played patriotic songs, or represented various branches of the military. After lunch, all of the party barges that had been decorated to represent various aspects of American history lined up in the cove in front of their house to embark on a voyage around the lake. It was a delightful scene that I am sure would have rivaled any of its kind anywhere. Banners flew, patriotic music blared, and pretty girls in red, white, and blue swimsuits graced the decks of the boats.

Any of my aunt's visitors were welcome to ride on their barge if they would agree to wear a costume that was provided by the house. Some years, we were all in beach attire, and in others, we wore costumes that represented historical events in America. There was much hoopla, and red, white, and blue crepe paper flew in profusion. Stella and Danny won first place most of the time, but other members of the lake association gave them a run for their money.

There was an enormous amount of drinking that took place during the parade, so by the time the festivities were over, most of the barges returned to their own docks with their decorations hanging limply from the sides and their passengers a little more drunk than they were patriotic. My uncle would often miss the entrance to his covered boat dock and would bump into the end of the wall with such force that most of us had to hang on for dear life as he would back it up several times so that he could maneuver it to enter into the opening at just the proper angle. After many years of abuse, my aunt had the upper dock removed so that just the flat dock was exposed in the hopes that my uncle could get a bead on his destination without ramming into the wooden posts at each corner of the dock. Fortunately, no one ever was hurt during these outings, but his passengers were truly grateful to be on dry land at the end of each adventure.

My aunt didn't seem to have the same knack for housekeeping as she did for making money, so their living area was always in a state of disarray. Their home had once been a small cabin built on one of the most beautiful lots on the lake. Later, as they became more affluent, they had another bedroom, bathroom, and garage built on one end of the original house, making it appear much bigger than it was on the inside. Their front yard was very small and separated from the narrow street by a hedgerow that was occasionally trimmed by my uncle. A small path led around the side of the garage and onto a rolling lawn that ended at the edge of the lake. Uncle Dan took special delight in mowing his luxurious stand of Bermuda grass and pulling the weeds out of his bed of purple iris. He even cleaned the house occasionally and cooked most of their meats on the grill while Aunt Stella opened various cans of vegetables that she served in an assortment of bowls that never seemed to match. Her kitchen sink generally was piled high with dirty dishes, and her refrigerator was not a safe place to find a meal.

One would get the idea that appearing wealthy and prosperous wasn't her goal in life, but the walls in their bar were filled with pictures of them partying on vacations in Tijuana, Mexico, and other cities where professional football games were held. Before my uncle's drinking habits robbed him of a clear mind and good health, they attended many of the professional games with others who shared their love of the sport.

Aunt Stella babied her husband and tried to provide the comforts of home for him in the only ways she knew because she had no role models to provide that script for her to follow. I believe my mother set a good example for her in the way she ran her household, and my aunt seemed to have a certain respect for her even though she was highly covetous of Mom's ability to cook and maintain an orderly home. My aunt yearned for a family of her own, but owning a dog was the closest she ever came to having something besides my uncle to care for. He was a magnificent black Scotch terrier and provided company for both my aunt and uncle for many years. I believe that he died of natural causes because after many years of being a part of their family he was just never there anymore when we visited, and no one told us children where he went. Perhaps the subject was too painful for Stella or Danny to talk about, and we were instructed not to ask.

The dark paneling on their walls served as a backdrop for my uncle's antique rifle, which hung over the entrance to their living room. Its silver stock was etched in the most beautiful designs, and I wonder where my cousin placed it in her home because I'm sure she inherited everything that once belonged to both my grandmother and aunt. The only thing I was given were nine blue plates that were part of an enormous collection of a limited pattern from Sweden, and this was only due to the insistence of my brother who happened to be with my cousin as she was cleaning out my aunt's house after Stella was sent to a nursing home for her own safety. My aunt insisted that Candace be the recipient of all her worldly goods because she felt a kinship with her that she had never nurtured in any of us. They are hanging in my kitchen to this day and serve as a reminder of those days we spent at the O'Malleys' house on the lake.

Christmas was an enchanting time at my aunt's house because she always put up a Scotch pine tree that reached to the ceiling. There were so many lights on its branches that it lit up the hallway leading to the living room, and there were bubble lights merrily clutching onto every branch. A roaring fire usually burned in the rock fireplace, and my aunt would always wrap an innumerable assortment of presents, of which very few belonged to my brothers and me. It didn't bother us very much that we would not be the recipients of many of those gifts because we had gotten used to the fact that our worth wasn't very considerable in my aunt's eyes and that our cousin and her family would probably be the ones receiving most of those purchases. We did enjoy seeing the pretty lights, however, and were given various assortments of Christmas sweets along with a few wrapped packages to place under our own tree to open on Christmas morning.

As my father drove away from my aunt and uncle's home after each visit, we three children strained to see the gigantic Santa Claus and reindeer that were perched merrily upon their roof. A myriad of tiny white Christmas lights lit up the sky around the decoration, and Santa's gloved hand waved a joyful greeting to everyone who passed by their house. I could not believe that my uncle was the one who climbed upon the roof to place the waving Santa on top of the slanting, icy shingles, but I'm sure that he felt like he could do almost anything with a pint of Dutchman's courage in his hip pocket and a wife who thought he was still the nineteen-year-old man she married years before.

There wasn't much to do in the wintertime at my aunt and uncle's house, so she let us look at some of the interesting items she had sitting on her shelves. I remember a little wooden man whose enlarged penis popped out when we pulled a string on his back. A wooden lady's dress flew up when we pushed her arm down as the front of her dress popped open, revealing an enormous set of breasts. She had a collection of cups that sported handles made to look like nude adults hanging on for dear life and other various items with sexual overtones. Mother usually helped my aunt clean up her kitchen during our visits while my father talked with Uncle Danny in his basement bar, so we were left to explore the living room instead of watching TV. We discovered that most of my aunt's collections of trinkets were not suitable for children but were drawn to the forbidden nature of these items anyway. Luckily for us, my mother took us to church and shared the Bible with us throughout our childhood, or I'm afraid that our experiences with the dark side at an early age might have primed us for a life of hedonistic depravity.

We seldom were allowed in their downstairs bar because my uncle had a large collection of antique liquor bottles sitting on shelves that lined each wall of the room, and he was always afraid that we might break one of them. Occasionally, we were allowed to open his refrigerator, choose a soft drink, and sit on one of his bar stools while he mixed his own drink behind the counter. His captain's hat would sit jauntily on the side of his head while he filled the drink with ice cubes and topped it off with a small umbrella or a bright red maraschino cherry. He never wore a shirt in the summertime, so his enormous stomach was always in plain view, and we children found it hard not to stare at the disfiguring scar on his chest. While the rest of his body was tanned a rich brown color, his scar was lumpy and pink and covered the entire section of his chest from shoulder to shoulder. Apparently, it didn't bother him that his scar was unsightly to most everyone else, so he continued to remain shirtless every summer until his body began to waste away with cirrhosis of the liver at the age of seventy-eight.

I can still remember the smell of that downstairs bar with the grass-skirt bar stools and hanging parrot that talked when my uncle pulled his string. It was a combination of dankness, beer, and a hundred other unquantifiable brands of liquor all combined into one unforgettable scent. I smelled it only one other time in my life, and that was in a downstairs pub in Amsterdam, where I half expected to see my uncle behind the bar mixing up his favorite cocktails with his silver cross hanging on a shiny chain against his scarred chest.

My aunt was proud that her husband was a former bull buyer in the stockyards, and she encouraged him to dress in cowboy attire. When he was at the lake, he was the captain of his yard, but when he and my aunt went out, he dressed in expensive, western-cut suits and leather cowboy boots. Aunt Stella would only buy him the best Stetson cowboy hats and long-sleeved silk shirts complete with diamond cuff links and brightly colored silk ties.

She also shopped at the most expensive stores in town for her own wardrobe and demanded that the salesgirls give her all of their attention when she entered their department. She wasn't a pretty woman, and she didn't project a sense of fashion in her dress, but she did pay enormously extravagant prices for the dresses she intended to wear out with my uncle. She was short and rather thick in the middle like her mother, but her dark eyes were penetrating, and her chestnut brown hair curled around her face in attractive waves. She wore an enormous diamond wedding ring on her finger, but beyond that, she preferred rather gaudy and inexpensive bracelets and necklaces that she replaced often. When she wasn't dressed for an outing, however, she would usually be seen in a plain pair of polyester pants and a cotton shirt or a pair of baggy Bermuda shorts with a knit top. She believed in comfort when she came home from a long day at her cigar stand in the hotel and rarely wore makeup when she lounged outside on their patio.

On Fridays, they had a standing date to eat at the Savoy Grill, and if someone else was sitting at "their" table, my aunt demanded that they be asked to move. Usually, the waiters were clued in to the fact that the O'Malleys intended to be served like royalty, but occasionally a new employee would not know the protocol, and he would be publicly berated by my aunt, who afterward would bestow a rather generous tip upon all those who waited on their table.

Stella's temper ran rampant during even the most innocuous situations, which usually occurred because she wasn't getting her own way. She was amazingly strong even into her later years and didn't hesitate to take a grown man down with her sledgehammer-strong left hook. Her episodes of violence were things that old wives' tales are made of, and she appeared to be proud of her reputation that has been proliferated down through the years by the retelling of those stories. One of the more notorious incidents occurred in her later years when most women of her age were approaching a stint in the nursing home, and it involved Ramona, who was so shaken by the incident that it took several years before she could laugh at the episode.

My mother occasionally rode with Stella to the second-day bakery or to the bank where the vice president happened to be a girl I went to high school with, and through my association with her, my aunt felt important because she "knew" a high-ranking officer of the facility. On one of these infamous outings that resulted in a much-told story, my aunt had talked my mother into riding with her to Rothschild's Department Store, which was located in downtown Kansas City. Against my mother's better judgment, she agreed to ride with my aunt if they could run by the grocery store on their way home. Thirty minutes later, my mother and aunt were on their way into the city. Their shopping spree didn't take much time, however, because my aunt was frugal in spite of her wealth, and they were on their way back home quicker than expected. My mother was glad that her sister-in-law purchased a sale dress without even trying it on because she had not felt well after a rather rough bout with her heart the night before, and she was looking forward to lying down before she started my father's dinner.

When they returned to my aunt's car, the traffic had become unbelievably heavy due to the lunchtime hour, but my aunt didn't seem to be unnerved at all by that fact. She pulled out into the traffic as they headed toward their home. By the time they reached the overpass that was headed east toward their destination, the traffic was at a standstill, and my aunt had overshot the ramp that would have taken them in the direction they wanted to go. An irritated driver of the vehicle behind my aunt's car began laying on his horn when he realized that Stella had put her car in reverse and was bearing down on his front bumper. It did not occur to her that she didn't have the right to make an entire lane of traffic back up because she had overshot her exit ramp, and she was determined to have her way in spite of the impossibility of the situation. The foolhardy chap thrust his middle finger outside of his window and turned the air blue with a plethora of swear words one might hear on a particularly hot construction site.

Perhaps my aunt was nervous from the situation, or maybe she was just reacting in the only way she knew how, because she reached under her driver's seat, pulled out a Japanese-looking sword, and proceeded to open the door. My mother looked on in utter disbelief as my aunt stalked up to the car behind and threatened to stab the driver if he said another word to her. The poor man's eyes opened wide, and his mouth quivered as he hoarsely whispered a dumbfounded apology. Everyone in the cars around them were either laughing at the audacity of the old lady with the sword or locking their doors in case her anger might explode on them. Nonetheless, traffic seemed to part in front of them, and they were well on their way before someone was able to call the police. As far as I know, my mother never rode with Aunt Stella again, and her infamous jaunts became her own secrets unless it involved my father, who was usually the one she called when she had trouble on the road. This was just one of the incidences where her half-hearted attempts at being feminine were all but overshadowed by her unmistakably mannish mannerisms.

She loved sex, however, and gave us her secrets of how to have a happy marriage even though my mother and I were definitely not interested in what she and my uncle practiced in their own bedroom. I don't personally understand what my uncle got out of their relationship in that way because he was usually in a drunken fog and obviously wasn't feeling much pain or anything else by day's end. Even though my aunt seemed to be completely in love with her husband, however, she was drawn to the excitement of an occasional extramarital affair, and this seemed to be a pattern she followed throughout her married life. She was proud that she still had the power to attract various men to her bed and was determined to disclose the particulars of her affairs with my mother, whom she knew would not tell her secrets to anyone outside the family even though Ramona made it quite clear that she was not interested in hearing about these unscrupulous liaisons.

Several years after my uncle had died, Stella boasted of having a long-term affair with the husband of one of her friends who lived across the lake because, to hear her tell it, June just wasn't fulfilling her husband's needs, and my aunt was willing to step in and relieve his sexual tension. My aunt's lack of moral values allowed her to betray a longtime friendship and still be able to sleep peacefully at night. Milton took their secret to the grave, and afterward, my aunt and uncle severed their relationship with June. She was vivacious, energetic, and projected the kind of femininity that my aunt didn't have, and I believe Stella was fearful that Dan would be drawn to her in much the same way that she had been drawn to Milton. She wasn't about to let that happen.

As my aunt approached her middle eighties and my uncle had passed away, she continued to look for someone to fulfill her sexual fantasies. My older brother and I had flown to town for a visit with our mother several months after my father's passing, and together, we decided to pay our aunt a visit. We knocked on the back door, and our aunt appeared with a fresh hairdo and makeup on her face. She asked us if we would help her straighten up her unimaginably messy bedroom while she put a new set of satin sheets on her bed. We agreed to help her stash her mounds of dirty clothes in the clothes closet and sweep her cluttered rugs if she would tell us what was going on.

With a sheepish grin on her face, she proceeded to tell us that a former acquaintance that she and Danny had met and befriended years ago had called her and was coming into town. He wanted to meet with her over dinner and talk about old times. His wife had died several months earlier, and he decided to fill his lonely hours with travel and visits with former friends. He did not know that my uncle had been dead for several years but was quite pleased when my aunt invited him to come to Kansas City for a visit in spite of the fact that my uncle would not be with them. His plans did not include sleeping with my aunt, however, because when we saw the satin sheets wadded up in the corner of her garage several days later, she confessed that he had made a hasty exit when she answered the door in her new see-through nightgown. That part of her life seemed to be over even though she didn't want to accept the fact that she had long ago ceased to have the sexual appeal that most men are looking for.

When we cleaned up her house after she moved to a nursing home several years later, we found innumerable magazines that graphically depicted sexual activities of all types and were saddened by the fact that she had not chosen a more chaste life as a legacy for her nieces and nephews to emulate. Her natural generosity and wit were overshadowed by her lack of moral integrity and volatile personality, and I often wonder how successful she would have been both personally and professionally if she had tamed those demons in her life. I choose to believe that she would have been immensely rich both in God's blessings as well as in her personal relationships had she grown up within a family where she could have learned those values.

She lived to be nearly one hundred and four, but I did not see any change in her basic nature except that she became a kinder person in the last few years of her life. My cousin lived near the nursing home facility and made it a point to visit her at least once a week, and my mother and I visited with her whenever I came to town. She seemed genuinely glad to see us, and it was always painful to say goodbye because I wanted to believe that if it had not been for her lack of love during her childhood years, she could have been the aunt that I had always longed for. Nonetheless, she played an integral role in my childhood experiences, and I will never forget her colorful personality.

After Aunt Stella whispered her final good-byes to Grandmother Gus, she turned her back to the ornate casket and announced that it was time for everyone to leave because it was getting late. Personally, I was relieved to have a change of scenery because the situation was beginning to fall apart around us as half of those attending seemed to be in some stage of drunkenness.

My little brother reached over and reminded me that I had to go back to the house with my mother in a few minutes because we were leaving my grandmother's viewing as planned in order to prepare food for the visitors who had come into town for Gus's funeral the next day. His gentle tap brought me back to the realities of the job at hand, and I began to reach for my purse and coat before I motioned to Mother that it was time to leave. I walked up to my grandmother's casket one last time to look down upon the woman whose life had influenced so many others in any number of immeasurable ways. Her face looked almost peaceful, except for the pursed lips and furrowed brow that revealed the true nature of the woman who now lay still in death.

I shuddered as I remembered my personal experiences with the body before me that appeared much smaller in death than she had looked while still alive. There are no words to describe my feelings of relief coupled with those of a pervasive sense of sadness that my life had been so negatively impacted by this person, who was now being laid to rest in a satin-filled coffin. I wanted to ask her if she felt any kind of remorse for the ways she had emotionally abused me throughout my childhood, but it was too late, and my opportunity to question her had passed as quickly as death had shut that door. I wanted to tell her how much she had hurt my brothers and mother with her disrespect and cruel words, but all I could do was try to forgive her for her unyielding determination to break our wills and crush our spirits. Otherwise, I knew that she would have succeeded in her quest to destroy our family. I could not let that happen because another generation was being formed in my body as I stood there and gazed upon the face that was now free of the hatred that had once been focused on us. I smiled inwardly at the victory that belonged to my brothers and me because in our own ways we had risen above her level of debauchery and hedonistic living.

With a deep sense of peace, I turned to grab my mother's arm and direct her toward the front entrance of the funeral home where her and my father's car sat waiting for us to start our journey to their house. Patrick decided to catch a ride with our younger brother so they could stop for a beer on the way home and talk about those who had attended the viewing. My father had made arrangements to drive my aunt to our house after he and his sisters had a chance to share a few final moments alone with their mother. My cousin and her husband agreed to bring my uncle Danny to our house in their car so Dad and Aunt Stella could ride together.

Chapter Eight

As I maneuvered my parents' car through the Kansas City traffic, I turned the radio on low to calm the tension that had been building throughout the afternoon. I glanced over at my mother's face, which had relaxed into the peacefulness of a deep sleep. She had been more tired than usual in the days preceding the funeral, and I was concerned that she was overdoing it by agreeing to serve refreshments to Gus's family and friends. It was amazing to me that after all her mother-in-law put her through, she was still willing to give of herself unselfishly when no one seemed to appreciate her efforts enough to pitch in and give her a hand. I was very grateful that I was able to help her even though she had already done a lion's share of the work before I arrived.

My mind began to wander back through the years as we passed a row of two-story houses that were built in much the same fashion that my grandmother's was. Bits and pieces of what I had heard about my grandmother's life began to play in my mind, and I wondered how a person could get as calloused as she appeared to be without eventually having to pay the price of an ultimate sacrifice of some sort or the other. It didn't seem to me, however, that Gus ever had to account to anyone for her bad behavior. This wasn't a good thing, as I later learned, because if she had been made accountable, maybe her life would have taken a different turn.

She was born in 1878, in a time where chastity and self-control were considered a virtue, but apparently, from the stories told about her, she demonstrated neither of these. Her family was plagued by poverty and illiteracy, but beyond that, they had a daughter who became known intimately by many of the less-particular men who worked the rails. Her family lived near the railroad tracks in a dilapidated shack that housed a rather sizable amount of inhabitants, and the children were left to explore life on their own even though their mother was a deeply religious woman. As if the family didn't have enough to contend with, their only daughter, my grandmother, developed a bad reputation that preceded her wherever she went and was not accepted in most social circles. Her liaisons with an innumerable number of men led to several illegitimate births and money in her pocket in return for not telling their wives of the affairs.

Years before, her father had moved his family to Rich Hill, Missouri, in hopes of finding work on the railroad, but all they found in that little town was more poverty and fewer chances to make decent money. His wife, a beautiful woman from Kentucky, met and married him in Wichita, Kansas, and she shared his dream of providing a better future for their children than they had. Their sons grew up to be respectable fathers and husbands, while their daughter grew more and more hardened with the passage of time.

Eventually, her mother asked her to move out of their home, and it was then that she set up housekeeping with an older man who would later become her husband. Her road to Kansas City was fraught with betrayal, debauchery, and eventually a dead husband. The fact that she would someday be my grandmother is beyond my comprehension and lets me realize that God's mercy overcomes any generational curses that reach beyond the grave.

One of the first memories my mother had of my father's family took place at the funeral of his grandmother. Gus made a grand entrance even though she had not been invited and strolled directly up to the casket to place a single rose in the lifeless hands of her former mother-in-law. She smiled victoriously as she backed away from the woman who had stood between her and the lifeless body of her son twenty years earlier. After Mother questioned several of the guests at the funeral about the obvious disdain they had for Grandmother, she learned that the feelings of contempt were well founded because Gus had killed the dead woman's son with a lethal dose of strychnine when she grew tired of being his wife.

According to the guests at the funeral, Gus strolled over to the church the very day she had been let out of jail. With the audacity of a prostitute, she had walked directly up to the casket and, with a smirk, looked down into the lifeless face of the man who had agreed to marry her in spite of her reputation. Tears of anguish and frustration had coursed down the cheeks of his bereaved mother as she stepped between her son and his killer. Everyone in town, including the deceased's family, knew she was guilty except for the prosecutors who couldn't find enough evidence to prove that Gus had intentionally poisoned her husband and subsequently let her loose. She bragged to several of her lovers in the months following her short incarceration that she had intended to kill the bastard; but for some reason, she got away with murder, and no one in town seemed to care except for the deceased's family. This story had circulated in the town for months afterward until my grandmother finally felt that she had to move to Kansas City with her new husband in order to start a new life.

After hearing about my grandmother's history with the deceased's family, Mother was appalled at Gus's audacity in attending her former mother-in-law's funeral, but Dad was able to convince her that his mother had softened in her later years and that she would be no threat to their impending marriage. My mother was very young and trusting, so she continued to date my father in spite of the overwhelming evidence that he carried the genes of the wicked matriarch and that he would eventually begin to display some of the same characteristics that had driven his mother to become who she was.

My grandmother had long since denounced fashionable clothing by the time I remember her and chose to wear loose-fitting housedresses for every occasion. Maybe that was because she was a large woman and tighter dresses just didn't feel comfortable, or perhaps she had just gotten tired of taking the time to enhance her appearance because it had been years since a man had been even the tiniest bit interested in her as a woman.

The last time my mother remembered her being with anyone of the opposite sex was when two drunken sailors came stumbling down the sidewalk holding her up in between them. They were all three singing while taking turns holding the others up. My father and mother had been staying at Gus's boardinghouse after the lease on their apartment ran out while they saved money for their first Queen Anne home, so Dad was aware of his mother's schedule. My father had been waiting in the dark on the front porch swing for his mother to return as he held her rolling pin tightly in his hands. He knew that his mother hardly ever stayed out this late and was concerned about her welfare.

His ears perked up when he heard the out-of-tune singing coming from two blocks up the street. He cautiously made his way up the sidewalk toward the cacophony of sounds. The clouds parted, and a full moon poured its spotlight on the three actors in an impossibly surreal scene. My father held the rolling pin over his head and threatened to bust the young men's skulls if they didn't leave his mother alone and go back to the beer joint they had wandered away from. It didn't take either one of them long to let go of Grandmother's arms and escape into the dark, even though they had been so drunk moments before that they seemed oblivious of anyone or anything around them.

My grandmother wasn't happy at all that her son had run her young admirers away and proceeded to turn around to try to find them again. Dad held on to her arm and threatened to call the police on the servicemen if she didn't comply and willingly come with him into the house. After giving it some thought, she apparently decided that she would come into the house and sleep her hangover off so that she might be able to go out again the next night and find her drunken escorts.

As Gus stumbled into the house holding one shoe and wincing from the dark blue bruises covering the insides of both of her legs, she noticed the shocked face of my mother peering around the kitchen door. She threw her shoe at my mother as she uttered foul words under her breath and proceeded to stumble through the hanging beads that separated the living room from her makeshift bedroom that had been set up in what was once a dining area. My father asked her what she had been doing, and she smiled as she told him that she had more sex that night than she had in the last ten years and that she planned to go back the next night to start all over again. Disgustedly, he threw a soapy washcloth into her and demanded that she wash herself up before she fell onto her bed in a drunken stupor. The sopping washcloth flew back out onto the living room floor nearly as quickly as it had disappeared the other way, and Victor just left it lying there as a reminder to his mother of what she had done the night before.

Mother knew better than to discuss with my father what she had seen, so she made a point to use the bathroom and climb back in bed before my father came upstairs. Mother turned her back to him and pretended to be asleep when she heard him sobbing as he sat on the side of the bed. It was soon after that incident that Mother and Dad moved out of Gus's boardinghouse and into a house of their own. The incident was not discussed again as far as my mother knew. My grandmother wasn't accustomed to apologizing, so it is doubtful that she ever asked my father's forgiveness for putting him through such an unpleasant situation.

The three major players in my grandmother's long-term relationships didn't fare quite as well as she did in the end, and I am curious about how they must have felt about her lack of compassion toward them and their families. After her first two husbands no longer were a part of her life, her third, unsuspecting husband also died before he reached old age. His heart condition had worsened after they moved to Kansas City, and Ed had to be hospitalized on several occasions to correct a life-threatening medical condition. Grandma wasn't accustomed to waiting on anyone else, so her ailing husband had to wait on himself each time he came home from the hospital, which resulted in him not receiving the proper nutrition or bed rest.

On one particularly cold winter afternoon about two weeks after he had returned from an extended hospital stint, the house began to cool down enough for the boarders to complain about the temperature in their bedrooms, and Gus demanded that he go down into the basement and shovel coal into the hot furnace in spite of his weakened condition. She could have reduced the rent of several of her boarders in return for their services, but that did not cross her mind because she did not want to give up any money that would be spent for her own personal needs. She put her husband's life on the line for a few paltry dollars and didn't seem to feel any remorse when a concerned renter found him dead on the basement floor with the coal shovel still in his hands. The coroner arrived about an hour later and pronounced him dead from an apparent heart attack. Since there were no suspicious circumstances surrounding his death, an autopsy was not performed, and Gus was able to play the part of the grieving widow once again.

She did not prepare for the loneliness that would be her plight after his death, however, because all of the boarders were so disgusted at the callousness of her actions that they moved as soon as they could find other accommodations. They had been missing personal belongings out of their rooms for some time and had suspected Gus of rifling through their things even before this incident happened. This became the final blow in their relationship with my grandmother. She was never able to fill her house with boarders again, and I suspect that word had gotten around about her husband's death as well as the filthy conditions that prevailed in her home.

At this point, she seemed to direct even more of her unfounded anger toward my brothers and me because there was no one else besides her own adult children on which to focus her attention; besides, that wasn't an option. Her favorite granddaughter had gotten married and seldom visited her, which further fueled the fires of an unquenchable emotional pain that was growing in her heart. Aunt Maxine's visits became fewer and farther between as she filled much of her time in the local joints with her retired husband, and my aunt Stella's visits were mainly to see that she had enough to eat and clean clothes to wear. Gone were the days in which the three of them would sit at the kitchen table while Aunt Maxine rolled Gus's hair and sipped on her bottle of cheap whiskey.

My father would insist that we children stay the night with Gus when he and my mother would occasionally go out with another couple. Each of us feared her in our own way because as most children can see through the outside facade and into the soul of adults, we were able to see the evil in our grandmother. She strongly disliked the idea of having to babysit us, but my father didn't seem to take that into account, as he would practically have to drag us into her house. Mother's concern for our safety was an ongoing issue during these "nights out," and their evenings usually ended with Dad complaining about her lack of interest in him. Mother always looked tired when they came to pick us up because she had worried about our welfare instead of enjoying the activities of the evening and getting a good night's sleep afterward. Her fears were well-founded because as soon as our grandmother shut her front door, she threatened to punish us if we did anything she didn't like.

During Mother's frequent hospital stints, we were taken to Gus's house because my father didn't want to find someone to keep us in our own home. Her cruelty was at its peak during those times because there was no one else around for days on end to keep her actions in check except for my aunt Maxine, who seemed to delight in partnering up with her during these times in order to make our lives more miserable than they already were. Together, they thought up innumerable ways to make our visits unimaginably fearful and humiliating.

Aunt Maxine would perm my hair until it resembled the hair of the black children who lived on the next block and then sit back and laugh at how ugly I had become. They would take pleasure in fixing food that was inedible and then laugh when we threw it up after they forced us to eat it. They found it amusing to see me panic at the sight of a coconut head that they would periodically place in the dark shadows of the landing on the stairs after announcing that it was time for me to go bed. My asthma would threaten to stop my breathing during many of these manic episodes, and Aunt Stella would slip me a sip of her sister's whiskey in order to settle me down and open my swollen airways.

Years later, Patrick found that coconut head while going through some of my aunt's belongings and decided that it would be funny to surprise me with it as I entered the airport terminal. Since I am not a confident flier in the first place, I find it hard to relax until I am in the waiting car and on my way home. Taking that into account, one can only imagine the impact that my brother had on my already challenged sense of security when he unceremoniously brought that head from behind his back and shoved it into my face. I gasped at the sight of that familiar article of abuse and had to hold on to my mother's arm as the scenery around me began to spin in a sickening nightmare of memories. I couldn't believe the callousness of his actions, but I'm sure he wasn't expecting my profound reaction to his thoughtless joke.

He assured me that he was truly sorry for bringing back my sorrow over those memories from the past but didn't realize that they were still an issue for me to overcome. He had not received the brunt of their hatred as often as I had because he had developed a friendship with the boy next door, and they let him spend many of his visitations with their family. Michael and I were left to fend off the adult bullies, and we were too little to physically defend ourselves. Therefore, we hung on to the hope that our mother would soon be able to return to us from the hospital, and we would once again move into the light of her loving world.

Of all the incidents that happened at my grandmother's house, one in particular stands out in my memory. It was the year 1945, and the Japanese surrender aboard the USS *Missouri* officially ended World War II. It was also a year in which I was fighting my personal battle as a three-year-old child in my own war theater in the backyard of my grandmother Gus's two-story house.

A tall, weather-beaten wood fence ran the length of her backyard, which served as a buffer from the noise of the trash haulers who pitched garbage into the beds of their trucks from enormous metal cans. The once-erect fence was fast becoming a casualty of the passing of the years because it had begun to sag precariously in several sections, and Gus was not interested in paying someone to buttress it up. The only redeeming quality of her backyard was the colorful rows of hollyhocks that stood at attention while gaily flaunting their summer blossoms against the backdrop of the aging balustrade. To this day, whenever I see hollyhocks blooming against someone's fence, my mind floats back to that sun-drenched summer's day in my grandmother's backyard and the terror that gripped every nerve in my childish body.

Grandmother Gus and my two aunts had taken their usual positions at the kitchen table to gossip about the neighbors and other members of the family when they came up with the diabolical plan that would challenge my feelings of security for the rest of my life. After whispering to each other so that I could not hear, my grandmother told me to run upstairs and put on my white organdy dress that was normally taboo except for church. I loved that dress because it reminded me of the angels I had seen in my mother's Bible, and I wanted to look just like them. I slipped the dress over my head, buckled my shiny, black leather shoes, and bounded down the steps expecting to be taken on an exciting adventure. Instead, my grandmother's and aunts' faces were drawn into masks of evil that secretly spoke of what might actually be in store for me.

I nervously asked where we were going, and at that point, my grandmother picked me up kicking and screaming and locked me outside of the bulging screen door and into the backyard where Daisy, my grandmother's ancient chow, innocently stood with saliva dripping off of her dangling purple tongue. The three crones cackled at my terrified screams and shouted that the dog was going to eat me alive if I didn't settle down. I tore at the screen door until my tiny fingers bled, and black dots danced in front of my eyes as my lungs began to yield to a seriously dangerous asthma attack. Just as I blacked out, my grandmother lumbered to the door, shoved Daisy away, and picked me up from the rickety steps. My aunt Stella had already mixed up one of her famous concoctions consisting of bourbon and a myriad of spices that she used to cure an abundance of ills, including my asthma attacks. As she poured the strong liquid down my throat, I immediately relaxed and slowly fell into a deep sleep that not only erased any terror that furrowed my brow but left me to question if my terrifying trial had really happened at all.

As I look back now, my ordeal actually began the night before as my older brother and I played in the front yard of Grandmother's home while she sat on the front porch swing observing our youthful exuberance as one might expect a Nubian queen to oversee the subjects in her domain. It was a warm, summer night, and the mentally challenged girl from across the street was chasing fireflies with my older brother and me. My little brother had already been put to bed because my grandmother had grown tired of chasing after the fifteen-month-old whirlwind and was ready to assume her position among the various dysfunctional visitors who appeared unannounced each evening after the last rays of sunlight lit up the sky. On this particular evening, however, an ominous rumbling in the distance heralded the developing summer storm clouds as the moist, warm air pressed in against our bodies and soaked our clothing with a drenching sweat.

Gus had quite a reputation for making excellent

bathtub gin during prohibition and frequently offered her guests a glass of liquor made from one of her former recipes. I suspect that it was because of these rather generous portions of alcohol that the ribald comments flew between my grandmother and her friends more frequently as the night wore on. Max, the taxicab driver who boarded at Gus's, usually stood on the stairs as far away from my grandmother as possible and casually leaned against the railing. In spite of his protruding eyes and slicked-back hair, he radiated a kind of gentleness that was lacking in the other adults who gathered on the porch.

Jenny, another visitor, was the oldest woman I had ever seen, and she smoked a corncob pipe from which a greenish, pungent-smelling smoke curled into the air over her head. I never knew where she came from or where she went on those summer nights. It was as if she just appeared for a short time to cackle and puff on her pipe and then disappeared into the night. Her arms reminded me of twigs upon which enormous dark veins traveled from her fingers and disappeared into the sleeves of her various assortments of shapeless, cotton housecoats. Strands of her thinning gray hair always seemed to be working their way out of the bun on the back of her neck to form a frame of constantly moving tentacles that shook when she bobbed her head.

I tried to stay as far away from her as possible because she liked to grab my arm and look deep into my eyes as if she were reaching down into the depths of my soul. Her breath smelled like musty rags, and a faint scent of mothballs seemed to follow her whenever she moved. After a few summer nights' visits, however, Jenny didn't come to visit anymore, and I felt an enormous sense of relief when I heard someone say that she had gone to live in a place where old people went to be taken care of.

Other frequent visitors included my drunken Uncle Bill and Aunt Maxine. It was my aunt Maxine who grew tired of our rambunctious games and demanded that we sit quietly on the steps while the adults drank and laughed at each other's increasingly confusing conversations. After a short time of sitting still under the scrutiny of those who were looking for an excuse to send us to bed, we began to poke nervously at each other until we gleefully fell to the ground. Immediately, my grandmother jumped up off of her perch, grabbed each one of us by the backs of our shirts, and dragged us into the house. She marched us up the stairs and into the clothes closet in her bedroom and whispered to us that there were rats hiding in the dark corners that would nibble at our fingers and toes if we made any noise.

As she shut the door, the darkness was so complete that we could not see anything but a tiny shaft of light that filtered through the keyhole. As I peered through the hole, Grandmother shoved the ornate key to the closet into the pocket of her flowing housedress and picked the back of her dress out of her ample crevices while whistling a tuneless song. Before she left the room, she turned to straighten her deceased husband's picture, and without so much as a glance back at her young prisoners, she resumed her position of grand duchess of the porch. Later, when she returned to spring us from our cell, she was disappointed to find us laughing and apparently enjoying our incarceration. Gus furiously flung open the door and promised to administer future discipline that wouldn't be so entertaining. She especially indicated to me that I wouldn't be laughing the next time I got in trouble. My ordeal in Gus's backyard the next day proved her right, and I never laughed during her psychotic episodes again.

Our last overnight visit with our grandmother occurred after she moved into a smaller house in the suburbs. She had been frightened by noises during the night, and my aunt Stella felt that our presence would help her mother get a good night's sleep. We resented being used to relieve the fears of one who had so relentlessly promoted fear and unhappiness in our own lives but were not allowed to say no to our father when his mind was made up. My aunt Stella had talked him into making us stay, so we were sure that between the two of them our fate was sealed at least for that night.

We slept in the bed together and hung on to each other's hands as we waited for those noises that had been plaguing our grandmother. It did not take long for the noises to start as soon as the lights were turned out, and my brother and I were so scared that we did not sleep the entire night. As morning approached, we must have dropped into a fitful sleep because the next thing we knew we heard familiar voices in the kitchen and were instantly awake.

Aunt Stella was talking to a man on the phone while our grandmother listened, and we were appalled at the topic of her conversation. It was obvious that she was trying to encourage a man to come over and have sex with her mother, and we understood what they were talking about because we were old enough at that time to attend elementary school where those topics are discussed frequently and with much interest. My father and mother were both disgusted when we told them about what had happened, and after that, my aunt was never able to convince either one of my parents to make us stay overnight with our grandmother again. The sounds that my grandmother had been hearing were from an infestation of rats that had gotten between the walls of her house, and after my aunt hired a pest control company, that situation was put to rest.

Occasionally, I think of that night and am thankful that my father agreed to put an end to our overnight visits because my grandmother Gus began to suffer from dementia, and her ability to restrain herself from inflicting serious damage became increasingly questionable.

Chapter Nine

I had successfully negotiated the traffic across Kansas City and was pulling my parents' car into the driveway of their well-maintained, ranch-style home. Mother must have felt the car slowing down because she turned and faced me with sleepy eyes and a sweet smile on her lips as I pulled into their double-car garage. A song called "Memories" was playing on the radio, and I remember poignantly that moment in time when life seemed to suddenly stand still. She reached over and patted my hand as she thanked me for letting her sleep as I drove. It was always a joy for me to see her relaxed and enjoying her stolen moments of peace before my father came back into her picture again.

It took several moments for Mom to gather her thoughts and shake the cobwebs of sleep out of her mind, but as soon as I opened her car door, she was ready to begin preparing for our guests. She was very organized and, in spite of her constant lack of energy, was able to pull together a complete array of food in no time at all and serve it with artistic appeal. She had already cooked most of the food that would be served, so all we had to do was warm it up and place it on the appropriate serving pieces that had been washed, shined, and placed on the shelves of her kitchen hutch. Aunt Stella had ordered a bouquet of assorted flowers, and the florist's truck was just pulling up to the front of the house as we finished placing all of the cold cuts on the table. The brilliant colors of the assortment added a splash of much needed ambiance to complete our presentation of the day's fare.

Just as we finished our chores, we heard the hum of several different automobiles pulling into the driveway, and Mother instructed me to answer the door as she placed the hot food into the appropriate china bowls. As each visitor came into the living room, I took their purses and coats and placed them on the bed in the front guest bedroom while Mother guided them toward the kitchen and the delicious food that would sate their appetites and calm the tension that seemed to always be an issue in my father's family.

Great Aunt Cora and her brother, Uncle Harry, were the first to arrive, even though they had made a quick, perfunctory appearance at the viewing; and, after eating their fill of the desserts, were ready to leave before most of the other guests arrived. There was no lost love between the man who had taken my father in as a teenage boy and Grandmother Gus, so he may have felt a sense of hypocrisy over his presence at Gus's going away party and didn't want to face the rest of her family with those feelings in his heart. Also, he wasn't comfortable socializing with others who knew the reputations of him and his sister, so they waited only long enough to give their respects to my father and aunt before making excuses as to why they had to leave so quickly. My father was clearly disappointed about losing his mentor and tried to encourage him and my great aunt to stay and keep him company while everyone else engaged in what he considered trivial dribble. His imploring facial mannerisms and persuasive words fell on deaf ears, however, as Harry and his sister left as quickly as they had appeared at the dessert table minutes before.

This was one time that my father was obligated to stay and be sociable to his guests, and it took all of his inner fortitude to be civil until the last guest left for the evening. After making a cursory appearance, my cousin and her husband had taken Uncle Dan back to his house on their way home because he had long since reached the end of his tolerance and was ready to strip down to his pajamas and sip on a cold beer while watching TV in his bar. As soon as the last person left, my aunt fell back onto the divan and let out a string of curse words that would have been more appropriate in a beer hall. My father was taken off guard by her sudden outburst and angrily asked what her problem was. At that point, my aunt cried until it seemed that her heart would burst as she babbled something about losing the only person who truly cared for her; however, my father's annoyance at her lack of self-control seemed to bring Aunt Stella back to reality and the fact that she had better get a good night's rest so she would be at her best during her mother's funeral the next day.

Instead of lending a helping hand to my mother and me, she made a hasty retreat and left without even mouthing a silent thank you for all the work we had done. My father muttered something about reading the paper and quickly disappeared, leaving my mother and me alone to clean up the kitchen and put the rest of the food in containers so my brothers could eat when they came home later that evening. I was angry at Patrick and Michael for not showing up at the house to help Mom and me meet the guests but was sure that they were probably a little more tipsy than they should have been, so it was probably good that they did not come home until much later. After everything was cleaned and put away, my mother and I retreated to the living room and just sat quietly, taking in the silence of night. We were both tired beyond belief and, after discussing the events of the day, retreated to our own bedrooms, ready for a good night's sleep. I guess my father had already gone to bed because I didn't see him until the next morning at the breakfast table.

He looked up, and a half-smile tugged at his lips as he asked me how I was feeling. I told him that I felt a little ragged, but a good cup of coffee would wake both me and my unborn child up enough to face the day. I thought about starting a conversation with him about some of the guests who attended our get-together the day before but decided not to after his attention turned to the newscaster's warning about a war in Vietnam. A sound like sand being hurled at the kitchen windowpanes took my attention off of my father, and I groaned as I realized that winter was introducing herself early by hurling a thick cloud of sleet down upon the roads and driveways of everyone who would be attending my grandmother's funeral that day. Dad yelled at Mother to hurry and get ready to go before the roads got icy from the wintry blast while he fixed chains around his back two tires.

One thing I noticed about my dad was that he was always prepared for the worst, and today was no exception. Just as my mother appeared completely dressed in the doorway to the kitchen, Dad came up the basement stairs, wiping his hands off on an old rag they kept for such purposes. I looked at my father's side view and for the first time realized that he was actually a very handsome man. All I had ever known from him was anger, impatience, and a general disrespect for other people, so I found it hard to look beyond his insides long enough to really see who he was on the outside until that day. His strong jaw and full head of steel-gray hair complemented my mother's fragile yet feminine appearance. It was a revelation to me that day to see my parents in another light other than the man and woman we called Mom and Dad. My thoughts were cut short, however, as my brother appeared in the kitchen looking for a cup of hot coffee.

Patrick has never been much of a conversationalist in the morning, so I didn't bother to ask him why he and Michael didn't come home the night before in time to help Mother and me prepare for the guests. I waited until he had drunk his first cup of black coffee before I began my interrogation. Even then, he wasn't agreeable to explaining his actions and asked me to call Michael to find out when we would be leaving for the funeral while he poured himself a bowl of cereal. Mother had enough time to stick her head around the corner and remind us that the funeral would be starting in about an hour and that we had better get going before the roads became impassable.

Before I had a chance to dial my younger brother's number, a knock at the front door told us that he was already there and ready to leave for Gus's funeral. His wife was sitting in the car, and I motioned for her to come in for a cup of coffee while I got ready. Michael said it was too slippery for her to climb the stairs in her heels, so they would wait for Patrick and me in the car. I hollered at Patrick to get ready while I ran down the hall to put on my makeup and brush my hair. I had already dressed in the suit I was going to wear for the afternoon, so there was not much left for me to do. Patrick, on the other hand, was another story. He resented the fact that he had to go to the funeral in the first place and refused to hurry up.

I put on my long, black, wool coat and threw my white angora scarf around my neck before I gathered up the courage to charge into the icy blast of air that was pounding against my parents' picture window. After one last attempt to hurry my older brother up, I descended into the basement so I could avoid the icy front steps and leave the house by way of the garage. My brother jumped out of the warm car to grab my arm and help me into the backseat before I had a chance to slip on the wintry mix of ice and snow. I was greeted by the genuine smile and a shared laugh from my brother's wife as we commented on my older brother's inability to meet time constraints.

My sister-in-law was a petite woman with coal black hair and eyes the color of dark mahogany. She was my brother's second wife, and he was determined to remain married regardless of the differences in their temperament and ages. She was four year older than he and an extremely neat housekeeper as well as a sharp dresser. His drinking habits had already become an issue in their marriage, but she was willing to overlook those habits if he was willing to be faithful to her and provide a good lifestyle, which he was able to do throughout their lives. She and I talked about our father's family members and what we were expecting at the funeral that day while we waited for Patrick to appear at the garage door.

Fifteen minutes passed before he appeared with a cup of coffee in his hand and his unbuttoned overcoat flapping in the wind. We all managed to swallow our displeasure at his lack of sensitivity in possibly making us late for the funeral and began our journey to the McGuilley Funeral Home. The weather became increasingly intense the closer we came to our destination, so it was a surprise to all of us that we arrived with time to spare. Perhaps it was the threatening weather that cleared out most of the downtown traffic, but there were very few vehicles on the street besides us and a handful of other fearless travelers.

When we arrived at the funeral home parking lot, we noticed there was just a smattering of cars parked near the entrance of the building and realized that not very many people would be attending my grandmother's funeral. Most of my mother's family lived too far away to attend the funeral, except for Aunt Bonnie, who had planned to drive up and stay the night with Mom and Dad before starting back home the following afternoon. Unfortunately, the weather had gotten so bad where they lived in northern Arkansas that she could not even back out of her driveway because the snow had begun to drift higher than the tops of her car tires. It looked as if the only funeral attendees would be the immediate family and a handful of my aunt's friends from the hotel.

None of us really wanted to attend the funeral anyway, so we were relieved that there were so few people to have to talk to about our grandmother. The years of her abuse had left its mark on each one of us, and we were secretly happy that we would never again have to put up with her attendance at any of my mother's future get-togethers. It was beyond the call of duty to have to act as if we sympathized with our father and his sisters over the loss of a person who had never liked us.

My brothers, sister-in-law, and I walked arm in arm as we slid over the icy parking lot and into the warmth of the funeral home. My aunts, uncles, cousin, and parents were sitting in the front row waiting for the service to start as we took our places beside them. It was none too soon because the priest appeared by Gus's casket and began to say his prepared homily as soon as we sat down. I figured that he was a friend of my uncle's because his lack of emotion over the death of my grandmother was apparent in the way that he occasionally glanced at the clock on the wall during his talk. Afterward, the guests discussed who would be riding in the family car to the cemetery. It was quiet for a few moments until my father spoke up and suggested that we all take our own vehicles because the cemetery was located close to our homes, and the weather might get bad enough to strand us in the city if we waited to ride back to our cars after the funeral. Everyone agreed, except for a few of the guests who lived in the city and chose to return to their homes as soon as they could leave.

I thought it was appropriate weather for Gus's final ride because it would be fraught with possible danger and fear for those who would be driving her to her final resting place while she lay quietly on her satin bed, oblivious to the extreme weather conditions that threatened to compromise their journey. My brothers, father, uncles, and my cousin's husband all served as pallbearers, which wiped out nearly half of those attending the funeral, while the rest of us stood quietly at attention as the casket passed. Aunt Stella, Aunt Maxine, and Candace held on to each other as tears of pain and sorrow rolled down their cheeks. The rest of us were observing their grief as unconcerned outsiders might do while watching a death on the evening news. We had never been part of their inner circle, and that day was no exception. As the pallbearers came back to reunite with their families, my father went over and patted each of his sisters and niece on the back before turning toward my mother and signaling to her that it was time to go. The only feeling of sadness that I felt was that they had never loved me like they loved my cousin, and the time for that to happen was quickly coming to an end. Somehow, I knew the Lord would give me back those lost years, and I was able to detach from any feelings of longing almost as soon as they darkened my spirit.

My younger brother was the first one in our group to indicate that it was time for us to head toward the car, but Patrick was deep in conversation with the priest about where he could find a gay church in the city so that he might be able to attend services the next Sunday before he left to return to Dallas. The priest politely discussed Patrick's request until there was no one left in the funeral party and then excused himself to return to his own rectory to prepare his homily for the next church service. JoAnn and I had already started our trek to Michael's waiting car and were having an incredibly tough time keeping each other from falling onto the slippery pavement. I was especially careful because I knew that I might harm my baby if I took a tumble that would be as jarring as falling on the ice, so I was grateful when the familiar arm of my younger brother slipped around my waist to steady me as I stepped into the backseat of the car. After lending a helping hand to his wife, he turned on the heater while we waited for our older sibling to exit the side door of the funeral home. The car had gotten quite warm before we saw Patrick emerging from the building and wondered what had taken him so long to appear.

The funeral procession had vanished, and we were left to fend for ourselves without the police escort that was leading the others toward their destination. As usual, he offered no explanation as to why he had held us up so long, and no one bothered to ask because we were silently contemplating the risks that Michael might have to take in order to get us back to our side of the town. It did no good to harbor any resentment against Patrick's disregard toward anyone else because we had grown accustomed to the fact that this was the way he was, and no amount of discussion on the subject would change his behavior. We had clung to each other for too long to let our individual personality quirks ruin our relationship. His humor had relieved our tension and fear innumerable times during our childhood traumas, and for this, Michael and I would be eternally grateful.

Our car didn't slide until my brother cautiously drove out onto the main street of the city, and it was then that he realized our trip might take much more time than we had anticipated. That realization, coupled with the fact that Patrick's tardiness made our departure even later than we had anticipated, set up a tension between the four of us so that the only way we could find relief was through laughter, which our older brother so willingly supplied through his uncanny ability to see situations from an alternate perspective. After a few reflections about his own thoughts concerning the activities at hand, all of us were laughing hysterically, and the anxiety of the day had been relieved for the rest of our trek to the gravesite.

Nearly an hour had passed before we arrived at the cemetery, and the last of the procession was disappearing over the ridge as we pulled up to the casket that was being lowered into the gaping hole in the ground. Several cold-looking sprays surrounded the area, and each one of us sighed a sigh of relief when we realized that since we were alone we didn't have to pretend to be sad anymore. All my younger brother had to say was, "Good riddance," and then we were on our way back to the house and our welcome refuge from the wintry weather. We had anticipated a quiet family get-together for the rest of the night, but to our dismay, several cars were lined up in our driveway as we groaned in disbelief that anyone would continue to challenge Mother Nature by prolonging their drive home.

Upon closer scrutiny, we recognized Aunt Stella's Cadillac and Maxine and Bill's beat-up Ford Malibu. Also, our cousin and her husband's shiny Mercedes sat in front of my parents' house far away from anyone else's car. I was shocked that my father agreed to let his younger sister and her husband come to his house, but they had surprised everyone by being relatively sober for the funeral, and it probably made my father feel good to include them for that one evening.

My younger brother made an excuse that he didn't feel well and unceremoniously bowed out of the evening's activities. When he saw that Uncle Bill was at the house, it didn't take him long to decide not to visit further because it was he who had terrorized Michael when we had to stay at Gus's house. He had the habit of pulling out his pocketknife and stumbling toward Michael, declaring that he was going to cut his ears off. As if that wasn't enough to completely terrorize a young child, he would then pick him up and pretend that he was going to throw him in the "Paw Paw Patch" after taking a swipe at the side of his head. It didn't matter that he had his knife turned around so that the sharp edge wasn't pointing toward my brother because Michael knew that anything could have happened when Bill was drunk.

Gus never stopped these episodes because, frankly, she seemed to find it quite amusing when Michael screamed in terror while frequently wetting his pants. I tried not to worry my mother by telling her about all of the horrible things that were happening to us at our grandmother's house because she was so frequently ill. When I told my father, he just laughed it off and told me not to be such a crybaby. I felt very vulnerable in our dilemma until I started listening a little more closely to the minister on Sunday mornings about how God cared for me and realized then that the battle was not just mine alone. I shared my thoughts with my little brother, but he didn't feel the peace as deeply as I did during our times of struggle.

As I reached over the front seat to hug his neck, I knew that some of the same thoughts were running through both of our minds. I understood his misgivings about facing my uncle, so I didn't argue with him about leaving Patrick and me there to fend for ourselves. Because I was pregnant, I had a good excuse to retire to the bedroom after a brief time of polite conversation, and I planned to take full advantage of my condition. Patrick, on the other hand, didn't usually offer an excuse when he was ready to call it quits for the evening. He would usually yawn twice before telling everyone goodnight and then unceremoniously turn and walk out of the room before anyone had a chance to beseech him to stay longer. I was anxious to see if he would use this strategy tonight and wondered what Dad's family would think if we both chose to leave at the same time. Surely our presence didn't matter that much, or we would have been included in their private conversations that took place immediately after the funeral.

As Patrick and I climbed the basement stairs, we heard Aunt Maxine demanding to know what had happened to us while my mother made the excuse that I probably had to use the bathroom at the funeral home because of my condition. Before she had a chance to badger my mother any further, Patrick flung open the door that led to the hallway separating the kitchen from the living room and, with a great flourish, made a grand entrance. He looked straight at Aunt Maxine and, in a voice dripping with sarcasm, asked if she had feared for our safety since we heard her asking Mother where we were. She didn't know how to answer his question since her real motive for asking that question was to point out the fact that we were so much later than everyone else.

I followed my brother into the living room as I unbuttoned my coat and announced that I would return after making a hasty call to my husband, who had left a message earlier with my mother to have me call as soon as I returned to the house. He had heard about the nasty weather in Kansas City and was calling to make sure that I had arrived safely at the house before he went on his evening watch. We weren't able to talk for very long because it was time for him to relieve the man who was working the shift before him, and I had to return to the living room sooner than I wanted to. After making a few adjustments to my pageboy hairdo and applying a fresh coat of mauve lipstick, I made my second appearance for the night in Mother's living room. I wanted to make as little commotion as possible with my entrance, but all eyes seemed riveted on me as I quietly took a seat beside my mother on the couch. Aunt Maxine snickered as I crossed my ankles and adjusted my skirt so that my legs would be a little less exposed to their scrutiny.

My cousin broke the ice by asking how my husband was doing on his job and if I knew any interesting details about the upcoming election. Aunt Maxine broke in before I could answer her questions and announced that I probably didn't know anything because it was against the law for my husband to tell those kinds of secrets. I just shot her a scathing look and proceeded to tell my cousin what I had heard about the candidates and their families. Aunt Maxine sullenly asked where the coffee was and left the room while the rest of us talked about whom we were planning to vote for.

My brother followed our aunt into the kitchen and found her pouring something from a bottle into her cup of coffee. He caught her off guard because she hadn't heard him coming up from behind her, so all she could say was that my mother should have served some Irish coffee to liven up her dull party. "Maybe it's the guests who are dull and not the beverage," was all he could think of to say at the moment before she turned on her heel to leave him standing alone in the kitchen, pouring his own glass of wine. My aunt and uncle took turns leaving the living room throughout the next hour, so we all became suspicious that if they had earned a badge for good behavior, it would soon be replaced with the opposite.

While the rest of my father's family talked about the good times they remembered having with their mother, Aunt Maxine became more and more caustic in her remarks toward my mother, until my father brought her and Uncle Bill's coats in and asked them to leave before the situation got out of hand. I don't think he cared so much that she was insulting his wife but that it was getting past his bedtime, and he was ready for everyone to leave. Maxine grabbed both coats and, after throwing Bill's to him, told everyone she would see them in hell. She stomped out into the frigid blast of winter.

A pall settled over everyone else who was left, so one by one, they thanked my mother for her hospitality and left the house to be enjoyed by just our immediate family once again. Dad unceremoniously went to bed without saying a word while Patrick, Mother, and I stayed up to talk about what had just happened. It could have turned out worse, so we were all thankful that my aunt and uncle were willing to be on their way before a real destructive fight broke out between them and the other guests. After listening to mother's console radio and laughing about our own experiences with Dad's family, we all turned in for the night, grateful to be inside out of the raging wintry weather.

We had just gotten into bed when the telephone rang. My mother always expected the worst if a phone call came late in the evening, so she grabbed it with shaking hands and a pounding heart. My brother and I ran to their bedroom expecting to see our mother crying over an unexpected death in her family, but instead, she was shaking her head disgustedly as she handed the receiver to Dad. He jumped up and threw his robe on as he told Mother to hang it up after he went into the other room to talk without us hearing his every word.

As we sat on Mom's bed, we heard him shout several choice curse words and shortly afterward slam down the phone. He angrily stomped back into their bedroom and told us that Maxine and Bill were at the city jail because their car had slid into a ditch, and they were going to be booked for drunken driving if someone didn't come down and put up bail. He then called Stella and told her that he wasn't getting out in the ice and snow and that she should leave them where they wouldn't be a threat to anyone else on the road and would have a warm bed to sleep in for the rest of that night. She agreed, and my aunt and uncle had to stay in jail for the next several days because not only were they caught drinking and driving, but my aunt had called the policemen who picked them up every curse word in the book. Finally, after several days of cooling their heels in the local lockup, they were released to Aunt Stella after she paid their bail.

Stella had some influence with the local police, so their ticket wasn't nearly as much as my father had expected it to be. They didn't have to appear in court if they agreed to never again step foot in this part of town for as long as they lived. Their car had been impounded after it had been pulled out of the ditch, so my father and Aunt Stella paid to get it back to them and send them on their way after they agreed to honor the terms of their release.

Aunt Maxine had thrown her red high heels at the policeman who had taken her into custody, so because they had become a weapon, they were kept as "evidence," and she had no shoes to wear. The police gave her an old pair of used work boots that were several sizes too big for her and, before she had a chance to object, sent her on her way with a warning to be careful about how she treated the next policeman who might come across her path or she might be assigned a whole new jail wardrobe to wear as she served time in their correctional facility. Her usual perfectly coiffed hair and flawless makeup seemed to be left in the jail cell as she limped toward their waiting car with a red scarf tied around her matted locks and no makeup on her drawn face.

It was hard for my uncle to keep from smiling at his diminutive wife's condition, but he knew it wouldn't be in his best interest to let her see him enjoying her plight. He too had found the incarceration difficult to abide because of the cold temperatures of the cell and the body odor of his roommate, who had suffered nearly the entire time with the dry heaves. The food had been decent, but when he asked for a second cup of coffee, the sergeant snickered and asked him if he thought he was at the Ritz. My uncle's temper was kept in check, however, because even though his life with my aunt was fraught with indescribable turmoil, he could at least escape her endless harping with his old buddy Jack Daniels.

He limply shook hands with my father and thanked my aunt for her part in springing them out of the lockup. Then he went on his way toward the side of town where much of his behavior was overlooked by the authorities who still remembered his heroic reputation for fighting fires in their jurisdiction. He cautiously pulled out of the parking lot because he knew the police were itching for an excuse to arrest him again, and he definitely didn't want that to happen. However, as soon as he drove out of their city limits, his foot hit the gas pedal, and he and my aunt were on their way much faster than the speed limit would officially allow them to drive.

My aunt was delighted that her husband was so unafraid to break the law and encouraged him to speed even faster. Midway in their journey, however, a moment of sanity settled on Uncle Bill, and he slowed their charging rattletrap down to an acceptable speed. Maybe it was his aversion to doing anything that would delight his wife or an inner intuition that prompted him to slow down, but nonetheless, it happened at just the right time, because as they rounded the bend a police car was waiting on the side of the road to give a ticket to the next unwary heavy-footed racer. After warning my aunt to keep her eyes on the road ahead, he stealthily drove past another hurdle that could have been the obstacle that prevented him from depositing his wife at their house before making his way to the local pub.

For years, my brothers and I were fascinated by stories generated out of their explosive conduct, but it wasn't until I began to write about my family that I realized the depth of the shallowness of their lives. I realize again the miracle of my cousin as she went on to become one of the best operatic sopranos of Kansas City, and I am prompted to recall the verse in the Bible that states something similar to the fact that the Lord will "repay to you the years that the swarming locusts have eaten."

The rest of our visit was pleasant and without the usual times of tension that nearly always crept into our sojourns when my father was present. His inner turmoil prevented him from relaxing and developing any further closeness with his three children, so we learned to avoid his presence for any prolonged period of time. Patrick partied with several of his old friends who had come into town and stayed out several nights after the funeral, while Mother and I pulled out our family picture albums and talked about old times. I had stayed in contact with some of my friends from high school and college who still lived in Kansas City and visited with them when I felt that Dad needed a break from my presence. All in all, my grandmother's death was an inconvenience to all of us, but it worked for good on the other hand because it had brought us all together for a special time of bonding between my brothers and me. There were not many situations after that time that allowed us all to be together, so that was a gift that was not entirely appreciated until much later.

It is many years later as I sit here and look back over the years of my own life and realize how my childhood has affected my choices of professional and personal relationships. I smile at the blessings that were so liberally bestowed upon me as I made my way through the minefield of childhood abuse and the realization of the finality of death as my mother struggled to overcome her serious heart condition. As a child, it had been a struggle for me to keep the lid on my own Pandora's box of problems because I was too little to develop the skills that would enable me to deal logically with these perceived life-threatening situations, so I have had to learn to deal with them as an adult in the only ways I know how, and that is to call upon God's help and the wise counsel of a knowledgeable counselor.

My sons, husband, and a group of loyal friends have also surrounded me with their love and acceptance, which have given me the strength to recall and write about circumstances that might be similar to others who are struggling to overcome the nightmares of their childhood.

I have placed a picture of myself as a three-year-old child standing in the backyard of one of my parents' homes on the desk beside my computer and realize that my childhood was not completely defined by the abuse my brothers and I received. In fact, I had my own battles to fight as well as my personal victories to celebrate, which no doubt were impacted by my experiences at Gus's house but not diminished by them. As I look closer, I notice the impish smile on my lips and the glint in my eye. My hair has been curled and brushed and fitted on top with a matching bow that picks up the color of my handmade jumper and smocked blouse. One would never guess by looking at my image captured forever in this photograph that I had experienced even one day of abuse, but looks can be deceiving, and I have been reminded of that throughout my teaching career.

My mother was artistic and used her abilities as a seamstress to dress my brothers and me in the latest styles of the times, so we appeared to be successful and well taken care of. She was a good cook and was able to incorporate our leftovers into incredibly delicious meals. A rather large freezer always had a place on the enclosed back porch of our several different homes, and we were fortunate that both of my parents saw the need to fill it with enormous amounts of beef and succulent fruit and vegetables that had been freshly picked in the summer months. My father, brothers, and I picked peaches nearly every summer, and Mother froze them to save for the leaner winter months when we yearned for sliced peaches on our breakfast cereal. Mouthwatering steak and fresh corn on the cob graced our table all year long, prompting my high school English teacher to question my honesty about having steak twice a week as I had written in one of my essays for his class. It was a common occurrence at our house to be served meals that were normally found on the tables of many of my wealthier friends, but because of my parents' mutual agreement to find as many ways as possible to cut our food costs while serving us with nutritious meals, we were able to eat well all during our childhood years.

One of my favorite meals was the fresh boiled shrimp that my father cooked on Friday nights before he and my mother ran us by the theater on their way to go grocery shopping. I remember him bringing Mother's big, old, metal pot inside from off the garage shelf and filling it with seasonings and enough shrimp to feed the crowd at the Forum Cafeteria. Mother prepared a shrimp sauce out of ketchup and horseradish that was out of this world and served it in a bowl that was surrounded by Nabisco crackers and slices of cheddar cheese. She made the most delicious key lime pie topped with mounds of fresh whipped cream to complete the meal. Afterward, my brothers and I carried our dishes to the kitchen while Mother laid them in a sink full of hot, soapy water to soak until we returned from our Friday night activities.

It would have been great family fun, except my father could never just break down and enjoy the moment.

Instead, he was usually tense and ready to reprimand us for any tiny infraction of his enormous list of unwritten rules. It was as if he wanted to do all of the things that he had heard about other husbands and fathers doing for their families, but he just couldn't completely buy into the total idea of parenthood. Nonetheless, we ate our shrimp and raced to wash our hands before getting ready for the movies. Dad was usually sitting in the car waiting for us to get there, so we were working on an adrenaline rush even before he backed out of the driveway.

The smell of shrimp lay heavy in the air surrounding our family, and I'm sure the other kids made remarks about how they could smell us before we even took our seats in the theater. That didn't seem to be an issue with many of our schoolmates, however, because as soon as my brothers and I arrived, there was a bum's rush to sit as close to us as they could. My older brother had an unusually keen sense of humor at an early age, and the other children loved to laugh at his comments during the movie.

We were all in elementary school during these years of the Friday night movie adventure, but none of our parents ever seemed to worry about our safety or who we would be sitting with during the film. We were each given enough money to buy popcorn and a soft drink, and that had to last us for the entire show. The movie house was located on the main street that sliced through the small town of Englewood. There was a large, stone church on one corner of the downtown area and an assortment of various dry goods stores lining both sides of the remainder of the street. The theater was situated right in the middle of a group of stores, and if we got out of the show before our parents arrived to pick us up, we window shopped and talked about how we could save enough money to buy those wonderful toys we saw so enticingly presented behind the shiny glass windows. If my parents took even longer than usual, my younger brother and his friends would run races up and down the sidewalk, much to my older brother's embarrassment.

I wasn't as self-confident as my brothers, so I never let them out of my sight when we were left to fend for ourselves. This caused many squabbles because they had their own itinerary, and they didn't always want their sister tagging along. In spite of their reticence at having me around, however, I think I might have kept them out of trouble on several occasions because I tattled on them when I thought they were being bad, and that seemed to be a deterrent to many of their dubious plans. I remember one especially severe scolding that my older brother received because of my tattling, but I still feel that he deserved it to this day.

There was an incredibly scary movie showing on a stormy summer's night entitled *The Thing*, in which a frozen monster was thawed out and his hand continued to move after it was severed from his body. During the most frightening part of the movie, I became so scared that I crawled under my seat, closed my eyes, and plugged up my ears. My older brother, Patrick, became angry that I was acting so childish and grabbed the back of my neck while hollering out, "The hand has got you!" I embarrassed him beyond comprehension as I let out an incredibly bloodcurdling scream that scared all of the smaller children in the theater. The usher ran down the aisle to find out what was wrong, and after explaining what had happened, he led me by the hand to the concession stand and loaded me down with several boxes of candy, which I doled out to everyone else except my brother.

On every Tuesday and Saturday afternoon, there was a children's league that met in the bowling alley situated within walking distance of our house. It was nestled in the middle of a group of stores that lined the street in another little town called Maywood. Maywood, Englewood, and Fairmont were all small boroughs that bordered upon the city limits of Independence, which was fondly known as Harry S. Truman's town.

Several of the kids who lived on our street had been bowling for most of the summer and had asked my brothers and me to join their team for the late summer league. My youngest brother was the only one who was excited about the possibility of winning a bowling trophy for his team because he was extremely coordinated and very athletic. My older brother and I weren't the least bit interested because our days were already full of taking care of our animals, directing plays, and swimming at our aunt's lake house. Besides, my frequent bouts with strep throat and asthma kept me from being extremely excited about throwing a heavy bowling ball toward pins that seemed ridiculously far away. However, our mother thought that it was a good idea for Patrick and I to be more active and at the same time chaperone our younger brother. Reluctantly, I agreed to join the team but ultimately ended up looking forward to Tuesday and Saturday afternoons when our whole group of neighborhood friends walked or rode our bicycles to the bowling alley like conquering gladiators.

There were too many of us to be on one team, so we were divided by ages, and my brothers and I were on three different teams. I was one of the last ones chosen because I definitely didn't have the natural stamina and physical ability that many of the other children possessed. It didn't bother me to be chosen last, however, because every one of my playmates made it quite plain that even though they didn't trust in my ability to add to their team score, I was still one of their favorite friends, and that was enough for me to feel part of their group. I was going into fourth grade and already had experienced a lifetime of verbal and physical abuse, so any positive feedback was heaven on earth for me. That is why I still hold dear those friendships from long ago because they gave me the security and acceptance that I so desperately needed at the time.

After several weeks of bowling, I began to get the hang of throwing the ball and hitting the main pin squarely in the center. My score inched up each time we met, until I possessed the highest score of every member of the league, including both of my brothers. My team began to boast about being number one until the other kids in the neighborhood refused to walk home with us after we bowled. My heart broke over the chasm my good score was making between our team and the others in the neighborhood, and I told my mother that I was not going to do my best for the rest of the summer. My brothers were seething from jealousy because they never thought that I would do better than them; but when they heard me telling my mother that my friends meant more than my score, they both jumped in and told me that they would never talk to me again if I did less than my best. They even agreed to take up for me if they heard any unkind words being said against me in the neighborhood, and that was enough for me to keep going and ultimately win the overall best bowler trophy for the highest score ever made at the bowling alley for a child my age.

God blessed me with a good mind even though my health was fragile, and I suffered from abnormal fears of people, places, and situations. When I was four years old, I was reading children's novels, and by the time I reached first grade, my teacher requested that I be skipped to the next grade. My principal thought about it for a short time but rejected the thought after realizing that I would barely be the same age as the other students by the time school started that fall.

We had just moved back from California in the fall of my third-grade year, and I had a dear teacher who wasn't prepared for the extremely bright class that she was inheriting for that school term. Several of my classmates went on to become engineers, college professors, lawyers, teachers, artists, nurses, and even a rocket scientist. I personally became a teacher and ultimately received several degrees in my areas of interest in spite of my father's refusal to pay for my college tuition. My classmates and I weren't always devoted to our education, however, because even though Mrs. Williams did a good job of teaching, many of us would get bored after about the first hour of class when we had finished all of our assignments for the day and began looking for other endeavors to capture our inquisitive minds.

My mother still insisted on pinning a ribbon in my hair so that my matching ensemble of jumper, socks, and blouse would match and she could feel the satisfaction of sending me off to school looking like a young fashion plate. It was those bows that captured my attention during my long bouts with boredom, and after a few minutes of fingering and readjusting them on my head, they came unraveled and proved to be an excellent diversion from watching the flies mating on the windowsill. I would circle the ribbon and draw around it before creating my own picture in which everyone was happy and peaceful. Occasionally, I would try threading it between my fingers and pretend that I was a princess with many different silk rings. Sometimes, I would wrap it around several crayons and pretend that it was a gift for a special friend. Never could I tie it back into a pretty bow before the bell rang to announce the end of school, so I very carefully laid it in the bottom of my metal lunch box and told my mother that it had come off at recess or that a boy in our class had yanked it off of my head. I didn't want to tell her that it had kept me from being so bored that I felt like screaming at my teacher for not keeping up with the intellectual pace of our class.

On one particularly boring day after a traumatic weekend at my grandmother's house, the boy I walked home from school with snuck me a folded-up piece of paper when our teacher's back was turned. I noticed earlier that he was reading the encyclopedia and had a pencil and piece of paper lying on his desk beside the book. He was drawing something that he found quite interesting in that book, and I found out later what it was because a perfectly proportioned picture of the nude statue of David was soon revealed to me on that tightly folded sheet of Big Chief tablet paper. I stealthily opened the mysterious note and grabbed my mouth in mock surprise before sending it on to another of our after-school gang. I smiled at our sneakiness as the note passed from one student to another while our teacher was engrossed in listening to the red bird reading circle.

After a few moments of watching the reactions from others in our class, I decided to send my own creation to my best friend, who was the twin sister of the boy who drew the first picture. I was no match for this future professor of art at one of the country's most prestigious universities, so I was content to draw a stick figure of a girl with very large breasts. My friend quickly stuck it between the pages of her Nancy Drew mystery book before the teacher turned to focus her attention on her captured audience and start our lesson on the times table.

The future rocket scientist who had embarrassed himself the day before by waiting too long to go to the bathroom decided to boost his damaged reputation by soiling ours. As he smiled smugly at his betrayal, he raised his hand to get our teacher's attention before she had a chance to start grilling us on our threes and fours. Remembering the upheaval that was created the day before by Clarence's inability to control his bowels, Mrs. Williams immediately called on him to avert another possible chaotic situation. My breathing became shallow and my heart began to beat faster as his gaze fell upon each of my friends and me before announcing that we were passing nasty notes. My unsympathetic teacher demanded that each of us produce the note that had been passed to us and the name of the person who was responsible.

After shooting Clarence looks that could kill, we each reluctantly brought the incriminating evidence up to our interrogator and waited fearfully for her to pronounce sentence. She scowled angrily at each one of us as she opened our questionable works of art but then fought back a hidden smile that seemed to be twitching the edges of her lips. That was one of her idiosyncrasies that we had gotten used to during the year, but nevertheless, we were always confused as to whether she was mad or amused. Today was no exception, but we were pretty sure she was more mad than amused because she immediately sent us to the principal's office with notes in hand.

I was so frightened by what the consequences might be to our misbehavior that my asthma began to surface, and I found it hard to climb the stairs to Miss Noland's office. My other three friends seemed to be taking things in stride regardless of what was in store for them behind the principal's door. They had never been sent to the principal's office either, but they believed that Miss Noland would give them a second chance for good behavior. This wasn't the case, however, as she called each child in for a scolding and three swats with her "board of education," along with instructions to have a parent sign our works of art and return them to her the next day.

I had been sitting on the bench outside of her door and heard the outcries of the hostages who had gone before me, and by the time the principal opened the door for me to receive my licks, I had become so scared that I lost control of my bladder and wet all over her shiny wooden bench and oriental rug that laid underneath. She was either disgusted with me for soiling her office or realized that I wasn't emotionally well enough to receive physical punishment because she waived that part of my chastisement with instructions for me to have my parents sign my note and bring it personally to her the next day. Fortunately, it was at the end of the day, so I was able to walk home by myself without anyone else noticing the wet stain on the back of my skirt.

I had learned my lesson the hard way and found that crime didn't pay, especially for people who weren't accustomed to being underhanded. My ordeal wasn't over by a long shot, however, because I still had perhaps the highest hurdle to overcome. I knew my father wouldn't have any mercy on me and would probably administer punishment that would be far more severe than I deserved. I walked as fast as my legs could carry me so that I could get home before he arrived from work. As I ran up our front sidewalk, I was relieved to see an empty garage and prayed that my mother would sign my note without ever telling my father if I told her how sorry I was for being an embarrassment to her.

As I approached her bedroom door, I heard a low moan that alerted me to the fact that my mother might be sick again with her heart. I slowly opened her door and was shocked to see my mother pressing an enormous ice pack to her swollen cheek. As tears of pain slid silently down her cheeks, she motioned for me to come sit on the bed beside her. She explained through swollen lips that the dentist had pulled all of her teeth that afternoon and that he had placed a pair of dentures on top of her sutures, as was the practice at that time. She didn't have the money to repair her damaged teeth, so she chose to have them removed instead. My heart broke to see her in such pain, and I decided that I wouldn't bother her with my dilemma since hers seemed to be so much more serious. She sensed that something was not right with me, however, and asked if there was a problem at school.

Haltingly, I told her the whole story about how my friends and I had gotten into trouble and how sorry I was that I had drawn such a nasty picture. When I showed it to her, she didn't shout or tell me what a bad little girl I was; instead, she told me how sorry she was that I let myself be a part of such activities instead of studying my times tables or reading ahead in my social studies book. I asked her if she would sign my note and not tell Dad about my problem if I promised never to do anything like this again. She signed it and shoved it into my hand just as my father came into the bedroom to check on her condition. Fortunately, he didn't suspect anything, and as I turned to go upstairs and change my urine-soaked skirt, I glanced back to mouth a silent thank you to my guardian angel, my mother, who once again had protected me from my father's explosive temper.

The verbal abuse that was so much a part of my existence at Grandmother Gus's house had begun to leave its mark on my interactions with adults, and fear of the unknown began to take the place of childish abandonment. I was an excellent reader, but my real passion was drawing and painting on the easel because these activities somehow released much of the tension that I had built up after my visits with Grandmother Gus. My third-grade year was a traumatic one because I was dealing with a new school, a new neighborhood, and new classmates as well as my mother's poor health and my father's twisted family. I didn't realize that my reading and math skills were so far advanced from the rest of the class that my teacher was being pushed to find enough work on my level to keep me interested.

It was toward the end of that same year that we were given the Iowa Test of Basic Skills, and I passed with a post-high school score. The national headquarters sent an entourage of experts in test making to watch me take the test again while they observed behind the glass doors of my principal's office to make sure that I had indeed been the student who had aced their test. Without ever knowing why I was the only child who had to retake the test, I passed it with an even higher score, which created a new resolve within the test designers to develop a more difficult test that couldn't be cracked by a third-grader. Because no one told me why I had to retake the test in the first place, I was scared that my teacher thought I had cheated and perhaps was considering sending me to the principal's office for bending the rules again. It was not until I was grown that my mother told me about what had happened, and I wondered why she hadn't realized the significance of the situation and the impact that it might have had on my fragile self-image.

Years later, I had another chance to meet my former third-grade teacher in a class I was taking to complete my master's degree. As I was leaving the classroom after the first day of our course, Mrs. Williams ran up to me and asked if I had gone to Barstow School in the third grade because I looked just like a little girl she had taught in her classroom many years ago. I couldn't believe my eyes because standing before me, eye to eye, was the person who had nearly ruined my third-grade experience, and yet I felt no animosity against her at all. In fact, she seemed so thrilled to see me that I was sure she had forgotten all about my horrible day of infamy.

She announced to several of the other graduate students that I was the smartest child she had ever had in class and that I had aced the Iowa Basics Test while still a mere slip of a child. I noticed several condescending smiles as they tried to digest this bit of information, and then I imagined that one in particular was looking at me asking the silent question, "If this is true, then why hasn't she gone on to greater heights than teaching?" I have also thought about that several times and then decided that there is no higher calling than being a teacher.

Mrs. Williams and I were cordial to each other for the rest of that semester, but I could never get past her vanishing smile long enough to sit down and hash out old times. It felt strange competing for grades with a person who had at one time written an S for satisfactory on my grade card instead of an E for excellence in the area of deportment just because I slipped up one time in my school career. I got the last laugh, however, because when our grades were posted on the final day of our graduate class, mine was first in line and hers was near the middle of the list. She didn't seem to be upset over the situation, however, because in some strange way, she seemed to take pride in being a part of my success. We parted ways that day, but she will still live on as the teacher I remember most out of my entire elementary school experience, and I have the assurance that Grandmother Gus didn't succeed in destroying my ability to overcome.

Chapter Ten

When I hit the fourth and fifth grade, my grandmother's and aunts' verbal abuse escalated at the same time my mother's heart condition worsened, and I found it increasingly hard to concentrate in school. I was growing taller than most of the other kids in my class and felt awkward enough without members of my own family making fun of me. Somehow, however, my mother made me feel pretty in spite of their wicked words, and I was able to overcome most of their abuse by simply being a part of activities in which my special abilities let me compete successfully with other boys and girls in my class. For instance, I was able to express myself through art, and even though I was light-years away from my older brother's abilities, I was still considered a good artist for my age.

One of the yearly activities in Maywood was to sign up for a store window to paint Halloween pictures on, and I couldn't wait each year to choose my glass canvas. All of the young artists were gathered on the Saturday before the spooky holiday and were given the brushes, paints, and rules for decorating the city's business fronts. I drew the number of my favorite store, which sold books and stationery, and settled down to paint. Amid much laughter, excitement, and childish conversation, the windows were finally finished by day's end, and I was delighted at the fruits of my labor. Ghosts, grave markers, and witches graced the front of my store's window as I myself looked like a modern work of art that was covered from head to toe with all the colors of autumn.

While the children were instructed to clean up our messes, the judges convened after looking over each masterpiece and decided upon who would receive the trophies for first, second, and third place. I was sure that there was no way I could possibly win first place over my brother and several other truly gifted artists, but when the judges announced my name for the first place trophy, I cried tears of disbelief and stood ten feet tall as I walked up to accept the trophy that represented something much deeper than winning the contest that day. It was an affirmation that I was better than the cowering little girl who had been so ruthlessly mistreated and that I deserved good things to happen to me just like the other boys and girls who took these things for granted.

My mother insisted that I show my trophy to Aunt Stella and Grandmother Gus the next time they just happened to drop by our house, and I reluctantly agreed even though I knew that they were more interested in what Mother had prepared for lunch. I lovingly took my bronze and wood prize down from the shelf in Michael's and my bedroom and started down the steps toward certain rejection. It wasn't in my nature to boast about my accomplishments, so my discomfort over the impending situation interfered with my concentration, and my foot caught on the second step, causing me to fall the rest of the way. To my horror, my beautiful treasure flew out of my hands and broke in half after crashing onto the floor of the hallway below, and I fell into a heap of convulsing sobs.

Mother came running to my aid, but before she had a chance to console me, I ran back upstairs and cried until I fell asleep from exhaustion. Later, after Grandmother Gus and Aunt Stella left, she brought my trophy up to me in one piece. Miraculously, it was once again restored to its original beauty, and my tears of anguish were replaced with joy and gratitude. It seems that Dad had bought some especially strong glue the week before to complete a project in the house, and my mother used it to repair my damaged trophy and my broken heart. My aunt Stella must have felt uncomfortable over the situation because she and Grandmother Gus quickly ate their sandwich and left after giving my mother enough money to replace the glue that she had taken from Dad's tool box. In some childish way, I blamed my aunt and grandmother for the situation and made a mental note to ask my mother not to make me share any of my accomplishments with them again.

My father had never received a single music lesson of any kind, but that didn't stop him from trying to play every musical instrument he could get his hands on. It had been a childhood dream of his to take music lessons, but there was never enough money for such frivolities, so he was determined to learn the basic notes on his own after he became an adult. My mother also pined over the fact that she couldn't play an instrument, but she made up for it by her insistence on making us learn how to play the piano. Mother loved the Spanish music played and sung by Mexican performers in their colorful sombreros, and our house was often filled with the flamboyant Mexican music that drifted out of her highly polished console that commandeered a prominent place in our living room. When Mother wasn't playing her lively music, Dad was picking out chords on the piano as he listened to his favorite tunes. He even became proficient enough to play along with my California uncles as they played their steel guitars and bass, even though he swayed to the beat more than he struck the ivories in front of him. He especially loved picking out tunes on the enormous organ that he bought from a church that was being razed to make room for a newer building.

Our house either sounded like the Mexicans had landed or someone was having a funeral. Nonetheless, music was a part of our lives all during our entire growing-up years. Our weekends followed pretty much the same pattern until we became teenagers, and even then, we had to placate our father by picking out tunes on various instruments while he pecked away on the piano. On Fridays, we went to the picture show, leaving Saturday nights open for music.

Mother would fix a light meal before our musical

ordeal began and then take her place as our audience in the upstairs area that was shared by my brothers and me. Dad was often short-tempered during these sessions, so there was generally no laughter. Instead, the tension created out of my younger brother's and my inability to instinctively play my father's latest procurement usually resulted in tears of frustration and hostility among the whole family. It must have been hard for my mother to endure these nights of musical torture because she would usually make it a point to encourage us afterward while making one of our favorite snacks. On the other hand, my older brother was a musical protégé and as a result could pick up most any instrument and figure out how to play it before the night was over. He especially enjoyed the xylophone, even though his incredible talent surfaced through playing the piano.

My mother worked off and on throughout our childhood in order to provide the special opportunities that we would have otherwise been denied, and piano lessons for all three of us was high on her list. Somehow, my father talked my aunt Stella into helping out with our lessons, and we were well on our way to becoming the first generation in his family that knew how to play a musical instrument. My older brother learned the music so fast that he had completed the last of the Thompson's series before his first year of piano lessons was over. After learning the methodology and musical terms, his teacher provided him with opportunities to learn every style of music from concertos to the latest tunes, which he frequently played for audiences in various social settings.

Mostly, he delighted my mother by playing and singing to her while my father sullenly observed the joy that Mom obviously was feeling over the talent that her firstborn had been blessed with. I don't believe I ever heard my father tell Patrick how proud he was of his accomplishments, and I know that must have hurt my older sibling very much. Much later, when Patrick was pounding a flower arrangement holder onto Dad's freshly covered grave, he released much of his anger and frustration by shouting out a lifetime of unspoken hatred and concealed pain over his father's ongoing disdain for everything he represented in life.

My younger brother and I were not as blessed in the area of musical talent, and after several years of forced practicing while his friends sat and waited for him on our front steps, Michael was allowed to quit piano lessons. I, on the other hand, displayed just enough talent to encourage my parents to pay for continuing lessons with our immensely impatient teacher. Perhaps she expected me to miraculously display the same kind of musical talent that my brother possessed, but all I was able to do was excel at the same level as others my age. I still remember her enveloping my small hands in her larger, bony fingers and poking the flesh between my first finger and thumb with her incredibly sharp thumbnail if I missed a note. By the time my lesson was over, my hands felt like they needed to be wrapped several inches thick with gauze. Needless to say, this was a real encouragement for me to practice diligently so that my teacher wouldn't think it necessary to leave a permanent mark indicating my less-than-perfect performance.

Whenever she decided that it was time for her students to perform, my parents were united in their resolve to make me practice my piece. Patrick never had to practice as long and hard as I did because he perfected his pieces quickly, which freed the piano up for me to memorize my music. The only time he lingered to help me with perfecting my homework was when he and I were assigned a duet. I usually played the bottom part of the piece while he kicked me to catch up with his improvising. I disliked performing duets with my brother so intensely that I found myself making an enormous amount of mistakes during our recitals. He was able to exonerate himself later during the recital, however, when he was called to perform several highly complicated pieces by himself. He was truly our teacher's star pupil, and I was more than glad to give him the limelight because I was busy rubbing my bruised shins while he wowed the audience with his superb talent.

Somewhere between my fourth- and fifth-grade school year, a gigantic, black, shiny baby grand piano appeared in the sunroom of my parents' house. Suddenly, practicing the piano took on new dimensions, and I had to jockey with my brother to secure my time to practice. When we asked our father where the piano came from, all he would say was that our aunt had picked it up for a little of nothing. Whatever the reason for us receiving that beautiful monster of a piano, I appreciated the effort because I could picture myself as a concert pianist sitting down to play in front of an audience of hundreds of people who dressed up just to see me perform. My mastery of the piano progressed to newer heights as I took more and more time to practice, which ultimately prompted my teacher to no longer stick me with her sharp nail.

I was able to play in my Sunday school class as well as in my classroom years later, but most of all, those early experiences opened the door to me being able to play for my own pleasure. I still sit on the wrought iron piano bench that is a remnant from those childhood days and play the piano like I did in the sunroom of our house as my mother sat nearby in a chair, tapping her foot to the rhythm of the song I was pounding out on our baby grand piano.

Chapter Eleven

We were fortunate that Dad loved animals almost as much as we did and didn't mind us having a multitude of pets as long as they didn't interfere with his comfort. He was denied the joy of having pets as a child because his aunt and uncle were so poor that it was all they could do to feed him, his sister, and his older brother.

The other kids in our neighborhood were in awe of our never-ending collection of animals and insisted on helping us feed and care for them just as paid zoo attendants might do. In fact, I suspect my younger brother's friends might have even traded a candy bar or two for the chance to hold our overgrown furry white rabbit, Harvey, while my older brother and I cleaned his constantly messy cage. They weren't prepared for the injuries his powerful hind legs could inflict, however, so we almost lost Harvey on innumerable occasions when his young caretakers dropped him onto the ground.

There seemed to be an uncanny silent alarm that beckoned the rest of the neighborhood when we needed help to recapture our fleeing rabbit. We had a rather large yard, with many different plants growing in profusion, which provided numerous places for our rabbit to play "Hide and Seek." That didn't stop the resolve of the Maywood Street gang from trying to recapture Harvey, however, and after many boisterous afternoons of running, shouting, and clamoring after our terrified rabbit, we eventually wore down his desire to escape and almost always found him peacefully chomping on my mother's mint leaves growing on the side of our house. He would be completely exhausted after his unsuccessful escape attempt and showed no resistance to being placed back into his cage with his rabbit food and a bowl of cool water.

If we finished our chase before my father arrived home from work, my mother would bring us all a glass of cold Kool-Aid in her colorful aluminum glasses while droplets of water slid down the sides and over our sweaty hands. Sometimes there were nine or ten of us sitting on our back steps enjoying the togetherness of friends who had accomplished a common goal and sharing the rewards of a job well done. As soon as they heard my father's car turning into the driveway, cups were turned up to enjoy the last drop of their treat before they turned to say goodbye and return to their own homes to watch the *Howdy Doody* TV show and tackle their homework before eating their evening meal. Our father didn't make it a habit to stop and ask us how our day had gone, and we were glad that he didn't because his temperament was usually at its lowest level by that time. He was ready to wash off the dirt from the machine shop and settle in for the night without being reminded of the fact that the reason for his hard work was to provide for the three children who always seemed to be in his way.

Easter was the time when we made our annual trek to the feed store in Fairmont to buy our pastel-colored chicks. Aunt Stella gave us each a dollar for our weekly allowance, and we had saved a sizable amount in preparation for that yearly event. Mother provided each of us with our own shoebox, in which we poked air holes and placed a small pile of dried grass in the corner for the comfort of the newest members of our animal kingdom. The spring of my fourth grade was a special time because Mother allowed my brothers and me to walk the two-mile distance by ourselves.

We were familiar with the route because it was the same one we took every Sunday on our way to church, and we knew who lived in most of the houses on our way to the store. We hadn't gotten very far when familiar voices shouted out for us to wait for them to join us in our journey. Johnnie and his sister, Beth Anne, caught up with us just as we got to the bridge, and the five of us fairly skipped down the sidewalk toward our destination. Other kids from our school shouted out at us as we passed by, but we didn't tell them where we were going because we wanted the pick of the chicks, and we knew that the bigger schoolmates would shove in front of us and choose the healthiest chicks.

It was as if the Pied Piper had led children of all sizes and shapes to the feed store because by the time we arrived at our destination, children were lining up two-deep behind us to pick out their own Easter chick. The salesman behind the counter brought out the first wooden box filled with the little, cheeping, pastel creatures, and we each got to choose our own chick and a small sack of feed. My brothers and I chose different-colored chicks so we could tell which one was our own and then left with our new babies secure in their cardboard boxes and a sack of feed on top of each one. Our friends had forgotten to bring their own box, so we agreed to share ours with them until they got back to their own house.

We all took turns lovingly carrying our new babies while we talked about what kind of pens we were going to build in our backyards. The wind had picked up, and the skies were rumbling by the time we had reached the bridge again. We had been so engrossed in our conversations that we did not notice how black the sky had grown, and our houses were still several blocks away. All of a sudden, a bolt of lightning split through the air around us, and we all scurried to find shelter under the bridge just as a train pulling a full load of boxcars rumbled toward us.

The engineer had seen us jump under the bridge, but it was too late for him to stop the engine, so we all hunkered together in the crawl space directly under the road and hung on to our boxes for dear life as the train began to slow down. The huge metal monster was making incredibly loud screeching noises as it ground down to a halt, but before the engineer had a chance to jump out and scold us, we clung on to each other's hands and ran toward our homes. The storm no longer seemed as frightening as it had been minutes before, so we sprinted toward Maywood Street, oblivious of the enormous raindrops that were mercilessly pelting down upon us.

Our friends shouted for us to keep their chicks until they could come to our house and get them after the storm let up and, without saying a word, scuttled into their home while we ran the rest of the distance in record time. Our older brother ran ahead of Michael and me, leaving us to the mercy of the elements. The cardboard was beginning to melt from the deluge, and the seed from our sacks began to spill out onto the street. Miraculously, one of the elderly spinster sisters who lived down our street had noticed our dilemma and opened their door to beckon us into their house until the storm subsided. My little brother and I reluctantly agreed to take them up on their offer and raced up their sidewalk and into the parlor of their well-kept cottage.

None of the children ever trick-or-treated at their house because they did not leave their porch light on at Halloween, and we never saw anyone visiting them during the five years that we lived in that neighborhood. They were a mystery to all of the neighbors and especially to the kids who often thought that old people could possibly be witches and, at best, magical creatures who could read their future in a crystal ball. I remembered to ask if I could call my mother to tell her where we were, and the old woman didn't say a word but nodded a silent yes as she pointed to the old-fashioned phone sitting in its cradle on her marble-topped coffee table. Patrick had gotten into trouble for leaving us to fend for ourselves, but our mother was so relieved to find out that we were inside out of the bad weather that her anger had subsided toward our older brother, and together, they settled down to enjoy the newest additions to our growing collection of animals.

We learned that the elderly ladies' names came straight from the Bible and were instructed to call them Miss Deborah and Miss Rachel. They seemed to be too old to have such young-sounding names, but we agreed to mind them anyway because we had been raised to respect our elders. Miss Deborah brought two small quilts into the parlor and drew them around each of our shoulders while she placed our chicks into fresh boxes complete with a separate jar in the corner of each, containing what was left of our feed. Miss Rachel disappeared into the kitchen to make us some hot cocoa while Miss Deborah wound up a strange-looking record player complete with an interesting, flower-shaped apparatus attached to the top from which flowed delightful music. While the storm raged outside of their door, my brother and I basked in the warmth of our newfound friendships and promised to visit them frequently from that time on.

Less than an hour later, the clouds parted, and sunlight flooded into our new friends' house, erasing the shadows that had just moments before concealed their innumerable antique collections that filled the shelves lining their room. My brother and I stared in awe at their wonderland of fragile glass birds and forest animals while the sisters quietly smiled at our youthful exuberance. After Michael and I relished the last drop of our hot chocolate, we decided it was time to go home and color our Easter eggs before we sat down to eat supper. We knew that Patrick would probably have a pen ready for our chicks, so we were anxious to free our little birds and tell our mother about our new friends.

From that day forward, my little brother and I periodically dropped in to visit with Rachel and Deborah and enjoy their stories about how life was when they were little girls. They always had homemade tidbits to share with us and were willing to listen when we needed a friendly ear. I had a feeling that they were aware of the trauma that always seemed to surround our family, but they never mentioned anything about what they had seen or heard. They were always delighted to open the door to us and our friends and never acted like they were too busy to stop what they were doing to give us their full attention.

When they found out that my parents were building a new house at the end of my seventh-grade year, they called me over while I was riding my bicycle and handed me a beautifully wrapped box. Both sisters smiled as I gingerly untied the silky pink ribbon and opened the expensive-looking green box. I gasped when I saw that they had given me the beautiful, round, gold locket that I had admired throughout my visits with them. It had been a present to Deborah from her fiancé before he went off to fight in the war, and when he didn't return, she had kept it in its original box on her dresser to remind her of the love she had lost in her youth and was never able to find again. It was more of a gift than I could ever imagine because I knew that the feelings behind the present came straight from her heart and that she was blessing me with the most valuable object she owned. I still wear the locket periodically and feel honored that Deborah had chosen me to pass on this most valuable gift.

Spring wore into summer, and two of our chicks grew into a pair of glorious white geese. Unfortunately, Michael's chick died after several weeks of being in the pen, and we held a funeral service complete with a tombstone made out of plaster of Paris on which my older brother inscribed the words, "Here lies Chester the Chick." We placed him in a metal coffee can stuffed with cotton so he would be comfortable in death and added his body to the growing animal cemetery behind our garage. After a few minutes of properly honoring his death, we played a rousing game of tag and remembered our grief no more.

The two geese grew more and more cranky and made a habit of cooling themselves under our neighbors' front porch steps. They weren't like our other pets that could be taught to obey us when we called them to return home, so we were constantly shooing them out from their cozy den. Our neighbors complained that their droppings were making a mess on their sidewalk and that their friend had fallen and hurt his leg on the front steps because our geese had made a surprise attack on his newly shined shoes. Several nights later, our geese were nowhere to be seen, and Mother served us the most delicious-smelling meat dish. After eating the succulent meal, my father joked that we had just eaten our missing pets, and all of us ran from the table crying giant tears of shame for eating two pets that had been members of our family. Mother never told us whether or not Dad was joking, but she didn't speak to him for at least a week after that night.

Another one of our favorite pets was a chameleon named Al who rode on the shoulder of my sweater tethered securely by a gold chain and a tiny, bejeweled safety pin. Fortunately, it was a passing fad to buy these little lizards and watch them adapt to the color of the sweater on which they sat. I'm sure that many of these little creatures didn't live to see the dawn of the next day on which they were bought, but, as usual, our little guy lived a whole year and grew into quite a healthy reptile.

He crawled on our attic bedroom screens and enjoyed eating the gigantic green flies that seemed to congregate there. He got used to us stroking him, and, as usual, Patrick bought a book that told us how to properly care for him. When the winter months ended his hunting forays on the attic screens, we fed him lizard food from the local pet store. We had to place him in a cage during the nighttime hours because after the sun went down there was nothing to warm his favorite windowsill, and he curiously roamed throughout our room seeking a warm spot on which to lie. If we got too busy to lock him up before the sun set, we would worry about him until we spotted him lying on the windowsill the next morning. This went on until the winter months again kept him from feeding on the screen, and he disappeared without a trace.

It had snowed deep enough that week to call off school, and we were busy playing from dawn until dusk. Building snowmen, riding sleds, and having snowball fights took precedence over our responsibility to Al, and the guilt we shared after his disappearance was well deserved. After another week of missing our friend, Mother helped us pull everything out from the wall and search through all of our belongings. Every day after school, we would talk several of our friends into joining with us in our tireless search for Al, but it always turned out the same—no lizard. Finally, our homework began to command more of our time, and we had to give up the search for our dear chameleon. He became another good memory that could be added to those that we clung to during our mother's frequent bouts with her weakening heart condition.

We finally had to accept the realization of Al's death months later when we found him flattened between the pages of an enormous dictionary that had been thrown down onto the floor of our walk-in closet. Obviously, we hadn't been using that dictionary to help us write our papers, and Al proved that by his untimely death. He must have crawled between the pages of the book to keep warm and was trapped when someone unwittingly placed a stack of encyclopedias on top of his cozy retreat. Apparently, he met his untimely death not long after he disappeared because he was as dry and stiff as a piece of jerky by the time we discovered his flattened body in the A section of the dictionary.

Before the sun went down, we hurriedly dug another grave in the pet cemetery and placed Al's lifeless body to rest inside of an empty matchbox. By that time, the pain we had felt when he first disappeared was almost nonexistent, so we quickly covered his shallow grave with a handful of dirt and ran back into the house to eat dinner before Dad got mad.

My older brother especially liked birds, and he always seemed to be the proud owner of one kind or another. A birdcage usually stood at attention near the foot of his bed, and a never- ending collection of bird toys littered the floor. He had a small record player that constantly seemed to be churning out tunes from his favorite musicals and an easel on which he painted pictures, mostly of our pets, and it was all off limits to my younger brother and me. Of all the birds that took over ownership of that cage, a blue and white parakeet named Billy is the one I remember the most.

After hours of intense training with our brother, his vocabulary became as extensive as any full-grown parrot I have ever heard. Sometimes when our brother wasn't there, Michael and I would open the door to his cage and let him hop onto our fingers and peck around our nails. I soon lost interest, however, because when Patrick was home, we were never allowed to come near his bird. However, when Billy the parakeet needed to be exercised, my brother would let him out of his cage, and he would usually make a beeline to our side of the room and bombard our beds with his cache of pent-up poop. No matter how much we complained, our demands fell on deaf ears, and we were destined to be on Billy's itinerary for the daily release of his tiny, round projectiles.

Our house in Maywood wasn't exactly beautiful, but our mother was able to engage her artistic abilities and decorate it with a pleasant flair. There were many nooks and crannies where we played hide and seek and a huge basement in which we skated during the winter. One of the most important rooms of the house that provided us with a feeling of security was our attic bedroom. Our father seldom climbed the steps to visit with us, so we felt that we had some privacy away from his scrutinizing eyes. It was this part of the house that sheltered us from many of the storms of life as well as the bickering that always seemed to be a part of my father's personality. It was also off limits to Grandmother Gus during her frequent visits because her weak knees prohibited her from climbing the stairs, and for that we were grateful.

Michael and I shared the other side of the room. I knew it would be an affront to his masculinity to have my dolls and other girly things covering our beds, so I played tea party and all the other games little girls play in our enormous walk-in closet. Sometimes, Michael would even give in and be one of my guests if I promised to fill his tiny cup with red Kool-Aid. Most of the time, he wanted to play war games with my dolls, and I ended up giving in because his ideas were a whole lot more exciting than mine. I know my mother must have been concerned over our choices of activities because when she came upstairs to check out the perimeter, my life-sized doll would usually be tied up and blindfolded as we figured out strategic plans to release her from the Nazis. Finally, Mother announced that I had received my last doll for a present because she found one in a foxhole without her fingers after my brother and I planned and carried out one of our most daring rescues of the summer.

Our newest dog had willingly entered into our war and became the enemy after he attacked my innocent doll. After a few minutes of pelting him with pebbles from the driveway, our dog decided that our war games weren't for him, and he ran away yelping after one of our missiles missed its mark and clipped him right on the end of his nose. He wasn't the only one who had been inflicted with pain, however, because Michael and I had both retained lacerations during the melee, and my beautiful doll was without all of the fingers on her right hand. I expertly bandaged her hand before bringing her back into the house, but Mother didn't relent on her promise to forgo buying me another doll.

I guess it was because Patrick was older than Michael and me that he got to have half of the entire upstairs all for himself. It seemed more logical to me that the two boys should bunk up together in one half, and I should have the other half because I was the only girl in the family besides my mother. He almost always got his own way, however, because my mother would give in to his obviously persuasive arguments and honor most of his requests. Perhaps she felt guilty that she had been unable to shield him from our father's fierce temper and tried to make up for it by taking *no* out of her vocabulary when dealing with him.

My little brother and I were good company for each other when Dad insisted that no lights were to be left on after we went to bed. We both were frightened of the dark, and if we heard any kind of unusual noise or saw a shadow on the wall next to our bed, we clung on to each other until we fell asleep. Sometimes, I found it hard to breathe because my asthma kicked in when we drew the bed covers up over our heads and forced ourselves to breathe shallowly so the monster couldn't find us in the dark. We were especially vigilant after seeing one of the many scary movies we attended on Friday nights.

After we cleaned out our mother's supply of garlic to place on our windowsill, she insisted on my father letting us have a nightlight for our part of the room. That caused us to be a lot less wary of noises and shadows, but a new problem emerged as the parakeet reacted to the light by fluttering and talking until the early morning sun flooded our room. We all three were casualties of sleep deprivation, and after several days of one or all of us falling asleep on our desks, Mother fashioned a cover for Billy's cage out of one of Dad's old lightweight shirts. The problem never surfaced again.

Billy became another casualty of the Baxter household, however, because after a year or two of blending into our family's schedule, he escaped from his cage and joined the millions of birds who flew free. Patrick had been busy studying his new piano piece for the upcoming talent show at school and neglected to keep Billy's birdcage clean. My asthma had been a medical issue throughout my school experience, but the molted feathers and dried bird stools blended together to challenge my already weakened immune system. My father threatened to take me over to his mother's house to let her doctor me with some of her home remedies. Of course, I began to suffer a myriad of other symptoms when I overheard his conversation and pleaded with my mother to stop him from carrying out his plan. Maybe it was from the sheer terror of thinking about staying with my grandmother that my fever shot to an unimaginable high, and I ended up in bed with doctor's orders for complete bed rest for the next two weeks.

My mother must have spoken privately with our doctor about Gus's abusive actions because he made it quite plain to my father that I shouldn't be removed from my familiar surroundings or my own mother's care until I felt well enough to resume my normal activities. Dad was constantly worried about making ends meet, so another medical problem always meant that he had to come up with additional money to pay the bills, and he was willing to experiment on alternative medical remedies regardless of the severity of my problems. On the third day of my medically ordered bed rest, my father climbed the steps leading up to our attic bedroom to see for himself how I was getting along.

Patrick was practicing the piano and did not notice that our father was about to tread on the hallowed ground of our room. His hands froze on the keyboard as a string of expletives split the air above his head. It seems that as our father came to the top of the steps, a gust of wind from our bedroom window blew a mixture of feathers and empty seed pods right into Dad's face and nearly threw him off balance. He realized immediately that my brother hadn't been faithfully cleaning up after his bird and that my asthma had probably been aggravated by Billy's messy cage.

My mother bounded up the stairs in spite of her bad heart to see what had happened. She arrived on the scene just as my father was roughly yanking the bird's cage from his stand and was getting ready to toss it down the stairs as retribution for my brother's laziness in cleaning out the cage. With her jaw set and fire in her eyes, my mother demanded that he hand her the cage before he did something regrettable to widen the already unfathomable gap that separated him and his eldest son. With rubbery legs and heaving chest, she took the cage out of his hand and ordered Patrick to come and immediately clean up his bird's mess before he played another note on the piano.

For whatever the reason, my father seemed amused at Mom's indignation and calmly handed the object of his anger over to her shaking hands without saying another word. Without so much as a glance toward my father, Patrick lifted his pet's cage out of our mother's hands and walked toward the back door to do what he should have been doing all along. Mother followed him outside with clean newspapers in her hand, determined to get the cage as clean as it had been on the first day it came from the store. The incident had left her weak and unfocused, so her mind wasn't entirely on the job at hand as Patrick handed her Billy's empty water holders to be washed out and returned back to him.

For obvious safety reasons, he usually cleaned out the cage in the house, but that would not be a possibility that night because of our father's obvious anger management issues involving his gross lack of responsibility. Very carefully, he folded the dirty papers that had lined the bottom of the cage and pulled them out of the opened door while he kept his parakeet from flying away with his other hand.

Mother returned with Billy's clean water holders and proceeded to cut the paper liner just the right size to fit securely in the bottom of the cage. Patrick took his hand out of the cage long enough to let Mom slip the paper into the bottom before replacing the clean containers. Just as Mom withdrew her hand from the cage, Billy saw his opportunity to escape and flew by her hand and straight up into the sky. Both Patrick and Mother watched in horror as his dear pet soared into the sky with the skill of a professional aviator, and we never saw him again.

I had never seen my brother broken with sorrow until that day, and I will never forget the unending rivulets that coursed down his cheeks as Mother tried to console him in vain. He called out to Billy until the blackness of the night completely shrouded everything within a few inches of his eyes. Michael and I didn't say a thing to him as he trudged up the stairs and lay down on his bed without taking off any of his clothes and cried himself to sleep. Sometime during the night, we were awakened by the crashing of dishes and loud curse words and wondered what else had occurred to steal our family's peace. It was not until years later that I found out what happened that night because Patrick was afraid that the truth of the situation might be revealed, and he was not prepared to be at the receiving end of my father's unrelenting anger.

It seems that he could not get Billy out of his mind long enough to fall asleep that fateful night, so he began to formulate a plan to get even with Dad. He blamed our father for his loss because even though it was Mother who let his bird get away, he knew that if he had been allowed to clean the cage in our house, Billy couldn't have gone very far before being returned to the safety of his perch. He knew that Dad was a light sleeper and would wander throughout the house after a short time of rest, stopping only for a drink of water before returning to his bed. As soon as everything quieted down for the night, Patrick tiptoed down the stairs and headed straight for the kitchen while his breath caught in his throat and his heart beat wildly against his chest.

Dad had not made his way to the kitchen yet, so it was perfect timing for him to complete his diabolical plan. Very carefully, Patrick readjusted several plates and positioned a drinking glass so that when it was moved the other dishes would fall down upon Dad's head when he reached up in the dark to find his favorite glass. Just as Patrick shut the cabinet door, he heard the living room floor creaking under the weight of our father's feet and quickly came up with a plan to escape without being detected. He knew that Dad usually made his nightly forays in the dark, so he inched along the dining room wall until he circled around behind our father, who by this time was reaching up for the handle on the cabinet door.

Just as the stack of dishes came rushing out off the shelf, Patrick took that opportunity to sprint up the steps while the sounds of his escape were covered by the breaking plates. As far as I know, Dad never suspected that he was the object of a sinister plan and even helped our mother replace the dishes that were broken that night. Nothing was injured but his pride, and my brother's pain was eased by the fact that he had found a way to retaliate against my father's unfeeling demands.

Many of our dogs were picked up on the side of the road by our father, whose compassion reached only as far as his upbringing allowed. We owned every mixed breed of dog at one time or another and always seemed to be able to tame them into being an acceptable member of our family until the call of adventure became too strong, and they would escape to wander the highways in search of freedom once again. One such pet wasn't so lucky, however, as he became lethargic soon after moving into our garage and wouldn't let us come near his foaming mouth.

My father made us all go into the house while he threw a blanket over the little dog and forced him into the trunk of his car. He placed his shotgun on the backseat and backed out of the driveway and onto the road that would take him to the river, where he would end the ailing dog's misery. Our mother told us that Dad had to shoot the rabid creature or he would die an agonizing death as well as place everyone who came near him in danger. The river was far too many miles away for us to hear the gunshot, but a car backfired on the street in front of our house, and we all cried out in sorrow over the violent death of our dog in spite of our mother's insistence that the sound we heard was not our father's gun.

Our many other pets included a nervous Chihuahua who bonded with our mother and defended her against anyone who chanced to come near her in spite of the discipline that she so readily forced upon him. His membership in our family lasted about twenty-four hours after he chased my younger brother through the house and forced him to jump upon my mother's dining room hutch to avoid being bitten by the jealous intruder. My father called a friend whose longtime pet had just passed away and offered him the first chance at staking claim to our miniature watchdog. He failed to tell him that the dog had a questionable personality, and after his friend got bit several times on the cheek, the dog moved on to the dog pound, where his destiny was sealed.

We owned hamsters, outdoor cats, guinea pigs, and even an owl whose wing had been damaged when he flew through a violent windstorm. We raised lizards, snakes, mice, and even fed a baby squirrel until he was strong enough to go out on his own. Our obsession with animals never inspired any of us to undertake the grueling path of becoming a veterinarian, but that did not stop us from befriending an incredible aggregate of various forms of wildlife as well as the usual kinds of pets that complete a family circle. Being pet owners also provided us with an outlet for much of our frustrations that stemmed from the ongoing verbal and physical abuse that were so much a part of our relationship with the Baxters because our pets provided us with a welcome diversion from the reality of our situation.

Chapter Twelve

Perhaps our experiences with the many strange personalities we encountered through my father's family let us enjoy the children who didn't seem to fit the mold of what most people would call average because all three of us children seemed to attract unusually creative friends who fit in with our rather quirky sense of adventure. Each one of us brought our unique set of pals into the equation, and together, we all were able to make life an interesting adventure in spite of the secrets my brothers and I shared at Grandmother Gus's house. I walked home with three very special friends every day after class and spent many afternoons in the basement of the twins' home dressing up in tutus and dancing to the grand music of the great composers of the seventeenth century.

Gordon and Sherri were my very best friends, and we shared our dreams for the future as well as our plans to sabotage Bobby, the boy who always tried to put dead bugs down our shirts. I never thought it strange that

Gordon insisted on wearing a tutu just like Sherri's and mine because his dancing was extremely creative, and he could do wonderful things with his collection of many-colored scarves. His mother served us cookies and cocoa while we wrote plays and danced until we fell into a pile, exhausted from our afternoon of fun and frolic.

Gordon was artistically gifted and began to make marionettes to sell when he was a mere third-grader. His mother bought the supplies for his creations and contacted buyers for his finished products. By the time he was ready to start college, the money she had saved from his various artistic adventures paid his way into one of the most prestigious art schools in the country, and his future was set. But in the third grade, we were only interested in having fun, so we danced until we heard his father coming in the front door.

Mr. Wilson didn't like the fact that his son was comfortable wearing a tutu, so Gordon would swiftly change back into the clothes he wore at school and become the dutiful son who acted like science and social studies were the highlights of his day. The only time he seemed to be able to cut loose was when he was dancing with an unseen partner as we three swayed and leaped to the sounds of violins and trumpets reverberating off their basement wall. Our fourth friend didn't especially enjoy our afternoon dancing, so we parted ways when we came to her street, and she skipped on to her own house. She had already begun to develop physically and became interested in boys at an early age, so our idea of afternoon fun no longer held her interest as it once did.

On many Saturday afternoons after we finished our chores, all of our friends congregated at our house to swing on the industrial-quality swing set that our father had made at his machine shop and set in concrete at the back of our yard. Mary Beth, our fourth friend, liked to swing as high as she could and yell out an invitation to all of the boys to look at her patterned silk panties. My younger brother and his friends would gather around the swinging Jezebel in the hopes of catching a glimpse of her fetchingly feminine underwear. My mother didn't say much about her obvious displays of feminine trickery until she began to stretch out the elastic necklines of her peasant blouses in the fourth grade and invite the boys to take a peek at her "textile teenage tits." That was the last straw before my mother insisted that Mary Beth keep her skirt down and her blouse buttoned up or she would be banned from our yard. Mary Beth didn't want to miss out on any of the good times we shared, so, much to the chagrin of most of the neighborhood boys, she complied to the rules. Our thoughts turned to a myriad of other activities that did not include looking at her blossoming body.

We collected a dime from everyone who came to see our original plays and played doctor when no one was looking. We ate ripe pears that fell from our ancient fruit tree and ran from the yellow jackets that always seemed to be swarming around the rotting carcasses of the fruit that had already lived their best days. Our parents let us make a tent out of the old, torn screen windows, and we lay under a canopy of shooting stars while the locusts sang their summer serenade. We helped pick the succulent orange tomatoes from our father's summer crop and helped our mother turn the bumpy green cucumbers into delicious, sweet pickles that would be placed on our hamburgers throughout the winter months. Our mother made sure that we never missed church and sat with us on the front pew while our demonstrative minister warned us about hell and assured us about our rewards in heaven.

All in all, it was a childhood full of exciting adventure and interesting family ties in spite of the fragility of our mother's health and the abusive nature of my father's family. My childhood was unique beyond comprehension, even though I'm not sure that I would like to go back and relive it again.

Chapter Thirteen

Several years ago, I decided to journey back in time by visiting my grandmother's old house. I found her street and was surprised to see no trace of the two-story houses that had once stood on these trash-strewn lots that now lay before me. An assortment of low-income apartments had been built over the first half of the street, and the rest of the block had been cut short by a cement wall that separated the neighborhood from an extremely busy freeway. I parked my car and walked toward an empty lot that would have been approximately in the same area where my grandmother's house once stood. Upon closer examination, I noticed a set of crumbling cement steps that were almost completely covered by mud and debris. Broken bottles and blowing pieces of crumpled newspapers littered the ground around my shoes as I looked for some connections to my past.

After several hours of searching for long-lost artifacts, it was getting late, and I decided it was time for me to return to my car before darkness overtook me. Something inside of me felt relieved as I let go of those memories from the past, and as I turned for one last look at the place where Gus's front porch once stood, my eyes caught sight of something red at the back of the lot. A single red hollyhock plant stood tall against a sliver of a wooden fence that had once been part of my grandmother's backyard, and the tears of a lost childhood poured down my cheeks.

My experiences at Gus's house did not defeat me, nor did they rob me of my joy for life. In fact, I realized in those final moments of my journey into the past why I had chosen teaching to be my life's ambition. I wanted to reassure as many children as I could that they can overcome anything that tries to break their will and that they can achieve great things in life as long as they do not give up their hope for a better future. That single hollyhock stood as a tribute in my eyes to all children who, in spite of incredible circumstances, overcome the trauma of their childhood and grow into adults who give back something beautiful that will encourage the hearts of generations to come.

About the Author

Caryn Welles is a retired elementary teacher whose students were taught a wide variety of topics through her original units of study, which were written and designed throughout her teaching career to motivate and develop higher thinking skills. She holds a MA in Elementary Classroom Teaching and is certified in the areas of Gifted Education and Elementary Supervision.

In her first attempt at competitive writing, she won a first-place award in the 2008 Arkansas Writers' Conference for her short story entitled *Pepper, a Most Unlikely Pet*. Through her original children's stories, she has been able to teach history and social studies in such a way that her students' imaginations were challenged and their understanding of the world was increased in a multitude of ways. She and her students earned many awards for excellence throughout her teaching career, and she is currently mentoring students at a local elementary school.

The completion of her first book, entitled *Hollyhocks*

on the Fence, has been a dream come true for Caryn, and her sequel, entitled *Growing Up Skinny Bones*, will be completed soon.

Caryn lives with her family in Little Rock, Arkansas.